Masterguide to Lease Administration

Lease Administration from the
Professionals

Compiled by: Peter D. Morris
CRX, SCLS, SCSM, SCMD
Greenstead Consulting Group
www.GreensteadCG.com

First Edition

Greenstead Media, Mill Bay, BC,
Canada

Printed in Canada.

287 pages

First edition: 2016

Masterguide to Lease Administration –First Edition

ISBN 978-0-9938774-3-8

Greenstead Media
2562 Kinnoull Cresc,
Mill Bay, BC V0R 2P1

Cover image provided by Pixabay.com

Contents

Important Notice to Readers

Laws are constantly changing. Every effort is made to keep this publication as current as possible. However, the author, the publisher, and the vendor of this book make no representations or warranties regarding the outcome or the use to which the information in this book is put and or not assuming any liability for any claims, losses, or damages arising out of the use of this book. The reader should not rely on the author or the publisher of this book for any professional advice. Please be sure that you have the most current edition.

This book deals with the business concepts, consequences and aspects of commercial real estate leases and commercial real estate leasing. Different laws in different locales will affect commercial leases, leasing and lease administration differently. Not all concepts outlined in this book may apply in your specific jurisdiction, given your governing laws. Although commercial leases are by their very nature legal documents, and the business practices surrounding the leases touch on aspects of law and legal regulations, the author and publisher are not providing any legal advice. The reader is strongly encouraged to discuss the concepts in this book with a competent legal advisor who is a specialist in commercial real estate leases.

As all leases have a financial impact on the investment in the commercial real estate, it is also important to consult with an accountant who is familiar with the specific accounting practices concerning commercial real estate. The author and publisher are not providing any financial or investment advice.

Introduction

This is a plain English guide to lease administration written for practitioners by practitioners from around the globe.

We assembled a group of senior lease administrators, lease abstractors, lawyers, leasing agents, accountants and senior real estate executives and asked them to share their thoughts and insights into aspects of lease administration and, in some cases, lease negotiation as it impacts lease administration.

In the following pages we touch on many aspects of the role of the lease administrator. But this book can't be definitive in itself. Why? The world of leases and their management is as varied as there are income-producing properties. There is the perspective of the landlord as compared to the occupier's perspective. Then there are regional differences concerning real estate and that is why we have included chapters from professionals in many parts of the world. Likewise, there are many different property types, industry practices and personal experiences.

As the editor of this book, with over 35 years of commercial real estate experience administering to thousands of leases as a senior executive and having worked in 8 countries, I can say with some authority that I still learn something new each and every day.

My belief is that once you read this book you will gain new insights into the role and the lease document. Perhaps you will shave years off your initial learning curve. It may be that as a result of reading this, you will formulate a new practice or system that will revolutionize lease administration.

Each professional contributor has written a chapter. I originally decided that their submissions would be edited to provide a consistent tone and feeling throughout the book. Not only did my editorial team find that difficult to accomplish successfully, we found we lost the contributor's unique voice and understanding (and dare we say passion) for their chosen subject. Therefore, aside from minor typographical editing I have provided their chapters as they saw to write them.

At the rear of the book you will find each contributor's bio. These are lease experts who contribute so much to our industry. Some additional chapters have been added by me, as the compilation editor, where I felt you would benefit. Those chapters have not been attributed.

We know we have just scratched the surface of all that is Lease Administration. If you are a seasoned lease administrator, commercial lawyer, leasing agent, property manager, property accountant or financial person, etc. and found something lacking in the scope of this book and/or having something you'd like to contribute to a future edition – and we are planning other editions – please feel free to submit your chapter to:

LeaseAdminBook@GreensteadCG.com

Acknowledgements

This book could not have been possible without the help and assistance of dozens of people from around the world who are as passionate about commercial real estate as I am. It would be impossible to properly acknowledge them all. However, I want to acknowledge our chapter contributors and the unselfish sharing of their knowledge. When the idea of this book was first floated, these professionals jumped right in without a moment's hesitation to offer their expertise and insights for the benefit of you, the reader.

You will find their bios at the end of this book. In reading them you will undoubtedly be as impressed with their credentials as I am. These people come from all around the world to give you a global perspective. They are leaders in the industry.

Chapter 1
THE LEASE ADMINISTRATOR

Congratulations! You have decided to pursue a career in Lease Administration........................ now what?
Let's start with the definition of Lease Administration. Wikipedia[i] defines Lease Administration as follows:

"Lease administration is a department that usually falls under an organization's real estate department.[1] Lease administration involves, but not limited to: receiving rents from facilities they own and paying rent for the facilities they lease. It has become an integral part of the accounting, administrative, and legal requirements normally associated with a real estate portfolio. Job responsibilities for lease administrators and real estate professionals include: lease review and abstracting, accounting and processing, lease audits, CAM charges, lease renewal options, repairs and maintenance, information management and reporting, occupancy cost analysis, operating expense review, and document storage and maintenance.

Once a lease is in place, lease administrators continue to manage and monitor rental payments, coordinate any tenant alterations, and handle lease amendments when necessary.

Depending on a corporation's departmental structure, lease administration or lease management can make up just one department under the umbrella of a corporation's real estate structure. Other departments may include facilities management, **real** **estate** accounting, construction, and **property management**.

Lease administration can be handled either internally or through outsourcing. The size of the organization's portfolio and the corresponding complexity of creating automated management and accounting systems are factors that influence an organization's decision to perform lease administration in house or to outsource the function."

Clearly, Lease Administration is a general term used to cover many specialized areas within the real estate industry. So, how do you determine which area you want to work in?

Let's have a look at a few questions that may help guide you in the right direction.

1. What do I expect from a Lease Administration career?

   In order to answer this question, you will need to decide if you are looking for a long- term career in Lease Administration, or if this is a stepping-stone to something else. For the purpose of this question, let's look at a long-term career.

   Ask yourself what, <u>exactly,</u> is it you are looking for?

   Are you looking for recognition as an expert in a specific area, are you looking to generalize, are you looking for financial wealth, are you looking for interaction with tenants, landlords, and other professionals, are you looking to gain expertise in software programs and spreadsheet creation and management, what about mentoring of junior staff/employees, are you looking for a lease accounting career, etc.?

Perhaps you are looking for all of the above, or are not yet sure what you are looking for? If you are not sure, do not worry, the answer will come with time and experience.

2. What are my strengths and weaknesses?

Knowing your strengths and weaknesses may help you decide whether you wish to become a general Lease Administrator, or specialize in a specific area. For example: Do you have an aptitude for numbers and math? If you do, you may find you are more drawn to the accounting side of lease administration, which includes account reconciliations, budgeting, percentage rents, occupancy cost analysis, asset and/or portfolio management and analysis, etc.

Ask yourself the following:
- What did I enjoy most in school, or during hands-on training?
- What provided me with the most satisfaction?
- What do I feel I'm good at?
- What do I know I'm good at?
- What do I feel I'm not good at?
- What do I know I'm not good at?
- What do I feel confident doing?
- What do I not feel confident doing?

- What would I like to learn more about?

Hopefully, after answering these questions, you may start to see a pattern of what direction you may wish to go in.

3. What responsibilities do I want as a Lease Administrator?

- Do I want to draft leases and other documents?
- Do I want to negotiate leases?
- What about renewals?
- Do I want to abstract?
- What about tracking critical dates?
- Records management?
- What about the accounting side?
- Do I want to have interaction with landlords, tenants, lawyers, etc.?
- Do I want to work in Asset/Portfolio Management?
- What about Property Management?
- How much responsibility do I want?
- Do I want the ability to make decisions on my own?
- Do I want to work on my own, or as part of a team?

These questions may seem overwhelming right now, however, they are key to determining what area you wish to specialize in, or, if you prefer to become a general Lease Administrator.

4. What kind of a company do I want to work for?

Do you wish to work in a real estate broker's office? What about a law firm? A property management office? How about a Landlord or Tenant Corporation? What about in your government's real estate department? What about an abstracting company?

Each of these types of companies have their own processes and ways of doing things, specific to them. You may find there are more processes and stricter guidelines to follow in your government's real estate department, than you would in a property management office or landlord corporation.

Lease Administration roles and responsibilities also vary depending on the size of the company. Many large companies have separate legal, accounting, records management, asset management, etc. departments, which specialize in one specific area of lease administration, whereas, a smaller company may have only a few lease administrators who complete most, if not all, of the lease administration roles and responsibilities on their own.

The answer to this question is all about personal choice; however, if you are new to the field, you may prefer to experience different types and sizes of companies to find the best fit for you.

5. Would I rather work as a Consultant?

    Working as a consultant can provide you with more freedom and a flex-work schedule, however, until you are established in lease administration, you may find yourself working long hours for extended periods of time.

    To work as a consultant, you require expertise, which you have gained over a long period of time, working in your specific area.

    For example: Abstracting – It would not make sense to advertise your services in lease abstraction, if you have not had extensive experience in abstracting. Some companies may prefer strictly abstracting of lease terms into a summary sheet or into their software program; however, the majority of companies prefer lease abstraction, which includes account review and reconciliation. If you are not familiar and experienced with CAM and TAX clauses and the Acts these clauses are governed under, you may find yourself in all sorts of predicaments, when attempting to reconcile an account.

Most consultants have worked extensively in numerous types of companies and gained all types of knowledge and experience relative to abstracting. For someone new to Lease Administration, it would not be a good idea to start out as a consultant.

"Lease Administrator" is only one of an exhausting list of titles used in the real estate industry to describe the roles and responsibilities carried out by Lease Administration personnel. The following is a list of some of the titles I have heard or personally held within the industry:

Lease Administrator, Lease Coordinator, Contract Administrator, Contract Coordinator, Contract Manager, Office Administrator, Office Coordinator, Office Manager, Leasing Assistant, Leasing Coordinator, Retail Coordinator, Retail Manager, Property Manager, Building Administrator, Building Coordinator, Leasing Law Clerk, Leasing Paralegal, Legal Administrator, Legal Coordinator.

The best of luck to you in your Lease Administration career, and may this book be a constant source of reference for you.

Chapter 2
THE ROLE OF A LEASE ADMINISTRATOR

When your friends ask you, "What do you do?" do you have a simple answer? Of course not, because there is no simple answer. A Lease Administrator can wear many different hats and have different titles.

In its basic form <u>Lease Administration</u> is the management of leases for a specified real estate portfolio. In this book we are going to refer to Lease Administrators, "LA", who are responsible for a Commercial Real Estate Portfolios, as opposed to a residential portfolios. They are jugglers, estimators, theorists, teachers, team players, collections reps, customer service agents, puzzle solvers, data entry operators, interpreters ... and sometimes even magicians. The number one function of a Lease Administrator is to work with your real estate team ***to increase the value of a real estate portfolio***.

The Lease Administrator can be responsible for several areas of commercial real estate and it varies from company to company and usually defined, as best as it can be, by your company's job description. They usually have a wide variety of education including, but not limited to, classes, seminars or degrees in business, accounting and legal. They have a unique set of skills. They are half property manager and half accountant. They are good at numbers and computers and can interpret and apply complex lease language to real estate databases. They are great communicators and can work easily with all personality types without propelling out of control. They are organized but can change direction at any given moment. They understand commercial real estate management, accounting and leasing. They know and understand property categories and lease types. They network and exchange information and ideas with other LAs. Lastly a LA is always a student. The commercial real estate industry is ever changing and one must keep up with the trends, changing markets and the expanding global economy.

A real estate portfolio can be a large mall in a Metropolitan Toronto to a small office building in a rural Kansas or a mixture of both. It can be one large mall or several small strip centers. A LA can represent the landlord or the Tenant. A LA can represent a tenant by managing a group of retail locations, an assortment of offices or a mixture of both. If you work third party you can also work with several different portfolios.

As you will find later in this book there a many categories of leases (mall, power center, retail shopping center, office building, industrial or a mixed use center, just to name a few) and have many types of leases (gross, net, full service, NNN or a mixture of these). On any given day a LA can work on maintaining their portfolio database(s), setting up tenant charges, complete monthly tenant billings, prepare a lease, review lease language for impact on cam recoveries, abstract a lease, review operating expense reconciliations, prepare an operating expense reconciliation and prepare challenges (or respond to a challenge), work on tenant collections, balance tenant ledgers, review charges that hit the accounts payable general ledger, revise expense accruals, manage and set up files, prepare operating budgets, prepare reports for portfolio reporting or due diligence for a possible purchase.

A real estate team can consist of a property manager, lease administrator, accountant and leasing agent or many different combinations of these. Sometimes a property management is its own LA or sometimes the accountant performs the LA function. A Lease Administrator can be part of many different teams.

So, as you can see each there is no canned definition of a Lease Administrator. A LA is responsible for a unique lease located at a unique property that is within a unique portfolio. They strive to increase the value(s) of the real estate portfolio(s) and play an important part of any commercial real estate team.

An Example
The LA needs to have a full 360^0 understanding of the lease from both the landlord and the Tenant's perspective. We worked with the tenant for a large commercial retail portfolio in Sacramento, California. We were responsible for reviewing operating expenses and challenging overcharges. In this case we believed the language supported our position that the lease allowed a 4% management fee but not an administrative fee or costs of management. Additionally, the lease expressly limited the tax recoveries. We drafted a challenge and clearly addressed our points, provided the language that substantiated our claim and provided the calculations for the corrections. Once we sent the claim then we regularly asked for

updates from the landlord without being too obnoxious. The outcome: we were able to save a tenant a substantial amount of money from the current year through the extension of their lease.

But why do I bring this up? Hopefully, results from your challenges conclude with saving your client money, but in this case we had a bonus. The landlord was so impressed with our knowledge, working ethics and integrity that they asked us to represent them as landlord, which we still do today even though the property has sold to another company. (By the way - there is no conflict representing the tenant and the landlord as we no longer work with the tenant due to a buyout of their entire portfolio).

14

Chapter 3
THE IMPORTANCE OF LEASE ADMINISTRATION

The way a team plays as a whole determines its success. You may have the greatest bunch of individual stars in the world, but if they don't play together, the club won't be worth a dime.
Babe Ruth

I'm going to make a statement that you may not have truly considered before. Lease administration and management is the single most important _task_ in any form of income producing real estate, whether for the owner or the occupier.

I know those in leasing, operations, accounting & finance, facilities management, development, acquisitions & dispositions, legal and even the corporate office may disagree and some may feel their _departments_ are the most vital, but let me explain.

I'll start with the comment that no one aspect of owning or occupying real estate is the end all and be all and my statement about the importance of lease administration and management may sound over the top. It takes an entire enterprise to be successful in real estate. That said, I believe lease administration is the most important _task_.

The Owner's Perspective
Let's look at what an investor really buys or a developer builds, in commercial real estate. I like the analogy of the wine bottle. The real estate itself is only a vessel much like when someone buys a bottle of wine, the bottle is only the vessel for the wine. The person buying the bottle of wine is more interested in the quality of the contents of the bottle rather than the bottle itself. While the bottle and label may be attractive to stand out on the crowded shelf, the person wanting to enjoy a good bottle of wine is really more concerned about the contents.

Likewise, the investor really buys the contents of the vessel and the developer builds the vessel for the contents. A beautiful empty building designed to create income is worthless to the developer and the investor.

The contents of an income-producing piece of property are of primary importance. The contents are the leases themselves backed by the covenants of the lessee. So the investor is actually buying the collection of leases and the ability of those leases to produce a predictable and desirable income.

Let's put this another way, imagine if you could buy a number of long term leases producing cash flow without all the issues associated with the property. Would this be an attractive, if not highly desirable, acquisition?

Right now I can hear the leasing department saying that they are the ones who found the tenants to lease, the legal department saying they created the lease, the accounting department stating that they produce the rent roll, the operators maintaining the building in the most effective manner, etc.

Income producing real estate revolves around contract management and every function in commercial real estate revolves around the lease contracts and the proper and effective management of those contracts.

The Occupier's Perspective
The occupier has a different perspective. Whereas, the landlord sees the lease as their primary form of income, the occupier see it

as an expense to be managed only as a part of their business.

That bears repeating in a slightly different way. The landlord's primary business is the bundle of leases; but the tenant's primary business is not the lease.

The lease is an expense to be managed by the occupier. More importantly, it is one of the single largest expenses a business incurs as a percentage of sales. The other two are: costs of goods sold, and employment costs.

Lease management is exceptionally important given the importance of the lease in the overall cost structure of the occupier. This is particularly true when the occupier also pays a recovery of property operating costs (often, and mistakenly, called Triple Net) as these fluctuate over the lease term and can make up a third or more of the total rent cost.

Unfortunately, in some instances, the occupier is so busy with all the other aspects of the business, lease management is not always appreciated for the contribution it can make to the bottom line; or, in some case, the viability of the business.

Both Perspectives
The lease defines the business arrangement and obligations of both the landlord and the occupier.

It is also about the transfer of business risk from one party to the other. Surprisingly, many often overlook this. After the lease sections defining the economic relationship between the landlord and occupier, the balance of the lease relates to the transfer of risk – and, it is typically the portion of the lease that takes up the most pages.

The landlord wants to transfer as much of their business risk onto the occupier. Conversely, the occupier wants to transfers as much of the risk associated with the location to the landlord. Here again, you will see the differences in each perspective. The landlord wants to transfer their *business risk* and the tenant wants to transfer as much as possible their *location risk.* Obviously, business risk seems greater than location risk. This is where the bulk of the lease wording negotiation occurs.

Lease administration and management is the cornerstone of the landlord's business. Lease administration and management is the cornerstone of protecting the occupier's business.

That is the overall importance of lease administration to both the owner and occupier as tasks. However, the ongoing proper management of the leases is equally important because laws and practices within the industry are constantly changing. Therefore, keeping abreast of these changes is both an ongoing challenge and an opportunity.

The Challenge
The challenge exists in the ability to keep abreast of all the new information. It isn't just new lease wording, but the laws and the application of new or revised standards, such as the new accounting standards in the USA and new technology. Sourcing, understanding and applying the new information and technology is an ongoing challenge and both owners and occupiers tend to give short change to providing resources to keep abreast, be it training or a robust research facility to be informed.

Another challenge is the lack of a unified formal training program in lease administration. This book and others in the series will attempt to address this shortcoming; but the challenge is persistent and widespread in the industry. For example, although various organizations have produced industry 'terms dictionaries', the people in the field across all aspects of commercial real estate co-mingle usage or have developed their own lexicon based on their lease wording and company practices. Add in similar terms in different industries that touch on commercial real estate and the problem is compounded.

Here are two examples:

"Asset Manager." Most agree that in commercial real estate an Asset Manager works for the Landlord or Occupier with the primary role of determining the strategic direction for the real estate. Typically, there is a lot of financial analysis involved but since the role demands overseeing the general performance of a portfolio of real estate, the Asset Manager must also be a real estate generalist with knowledge of the entire business cycle from acquisition/development to disposition.

However, some people refer to property managers as asset managers. In reality, the role of the property manager is the operational performance of one property or a few properties and the property manager's function is the tactical implementation of the strategy set by the asset manager.

But, in funds management, such as an institutional investor, an asset manager's role is different again as it is focused on equity management and the performance of the real estate's asset manager. The fund's asset manager may not have the commercial breadth of skills in commercial real estate that the real estate asset manager has, and the converse is also true as they both have a different focus.

"Operating or Occupancy Costs"
Either term, used generically, has many different meanings depending on what comprises the 'costs' as determined in the lease. Sometimes, the term includes property taxes and sometimes it doesn't, for example.

When an occupier speaks of Operating Costs of real estate may also include minimum rent and costs borne by the company but not paid to the landlord, such as direct utilities and premises insurance costs.

As a result, it is always important to refer to the specific definition contained in each lease and to clarify the meaning of the term in discussions and negotiations so everyone is on the same page.

The Opportunity
The opportunities are twofold.

The first opportunity is to the company. By staying on the leading edge of the information the company will be in a better position. It will be in a better negotiating position and in a better position in the industry by forecasting trends. This, in turn, reduces the risks associated with long-term contracts.

The second opportunity is for the lease administrator himself or herself. The Lease Administrator who is are the forefront of the changes in the industry is more marketable than one who is not. This provides more job and promotion opportunities.

The Single Source of Truth
Lease Administration is contract management and also information management, since the lease defines the relationship between the landlord and the tenant. Today's lease administration software is also tied to accounting and may also be tied to service requests, preventative maintenance, financing, project management and a host of other areas.

If you examine the architecture of modern lease administration software you will find it is built on the concept of creating a single source of truth, also known as a single point of truth (SPOT for short). In the SPOT architecture concept all data is kept in one central location. Any other reference to that data elsewhere only points back to where the data is stored in the one central location. This is done to avoid duplicate data points that could be missed if something is updated. One update to the central stored data would update all other places where that data is referenced.

In income producing properties, the central source is the lease administration software. All other functions such as accounting, finance, maintenance, etc. are all linked to this central database.

Anyone who has been through a process of migrating from one lease administration system to another understands the structure of the lease administration software. Aside from setting up the General Ledger at the corporate and property levels, all other information is in the hierarchy of:
1. Property,
2. Space (unit)
3. Tenant
4. Lease

Everything from accounting to legal to leasing reports, maintenance and operations is tied to these four items that are the responsibility of the Lease Administrator. As a result, it is vitally important that the lease management data is complete and correct. That is the importance of good, current lease administration.

Chapter 4
THE LEASE ADMINISTRATOR
AND ACCOUNTING

An important part of a Lease Administrator's ("LA") role is working with the accounting department. A LA's primary goal is to assist in increasing the value of the property (or the occupier's portfolio). The best way to do that is learn how a LA interacts with accounting and how their job affects the bottom line.

In some instances you will have a minimal role and in others you could play a big part. First step would be understand basic accounting and how a LA's role interacts with your company's accounting department. You need to have a positive relationship with the property or facilities accountant and have a constant open line of communication. Some of the tasks you may be asked to do are based on company's policy manual, which each company should have.

Your role as a LA could include:
- Input rent charges, set up recurring charges and rent changes, lease offsets and other charges:

Once you have the lease abstracted and the lease has commenced it is time to enter the information into your property database of choice. The current rent charges as well as any stated future increases should be entered. If any increases are based on the Consumer Price Index (also commonly known as the rate of inflation) it should be linked to your property database, if allowed. Make sure you are linking to the right CPI table (tables are sorted by area, by base, wage earners or urban consumers, etc.). If the property database doesn't automatically update your CPI increase then you should have a note in your system or on a calendar to trigger the calculation.

Monthly estimates for operating costs and utilities can either be entered based on the most recent budget or some property management programs will automatically calculate once you have the basic information entered in the property database (i.e. base year, prorata shares, denominator changes, gross ups %, exclusions, caps, etc.). This information should be on the lease abstract. If you are the tenant and you have not been supplied the monthly recurring charges you will need to contact the landlord for the information.

Other recurring charges can include storage, marketing funds and parking charges that generally have stated increases. You should work with your accountant on any other additional charges allowed under the lease to make sure they are credit to the correct income or offset account. Some leases may include tenant improvement reimbursements (usually amortized over the life of the original term of the lease). An amortization schedule of the reimbursement should be produced, attached to the property database and set up as a recurring charge. Some companies also track free or abated rent periods so check with your accountant on how those are handled in the accounting system.

You may also have other direct charges that are submitted to you randomly to be input into the property database. These can include after-hour HVAC, R&M charges or parking permits. Always check with your accountant as to where these charges should be credited on the general ledger. Some charges (i.e. after hours HVAC) actually offset expense accounts.

If there is a prorated period check the lease to see if it indicates a specific formula for prorating charges (i.e. 30 day months, 365 day year, etc.). A small thing but it can leave an annoying minimal charge on the tenant ledger if the parties don't agree on the proration.

- Process Move Outs:

There will come a time when a tenant moves out either by a lease expiration or an early termination. You should know a few basic laws for the area in which your property is located, one of which is how long does a landlord have to process and /or return a security deposit. Some local governments only include rules for residential security deposits but some include both residential and commercial deposits. If you're the Landlord and you don't respond to the tenant in a timely manner or with the correct information it could lead to some serious penalties. Once the security deposit is applied and there is still an outstanding balance you will need to work with the property manager and the property accountant to determine if it is collectible and, if not, what should be charged off? If it's collectible then one of the team members should take responsibility and work with the former tenant or legal representative on collecting the balance due.

How about tenants who move out before the end of the term? First work with your property manager and accountant and go through the process of closing out the account (which should be included in your policies manual). Ask the manager or accountant if the monthly recurring charges should be stopped. Then apply the security deposit and charge any outstanding charges (damages or partial year reconciliation). Calculate allowable lease up charges for the balance of the term (i.e. TI improvements and brokerage fees). The accountant, controller, property manager or legal representative should let the LA know how if the rent and additional charges should calculated for the balance of the term and posted to the tenant's account. Other additional charges (i.e. utilities, legal costs, etc.) should continue to be charged to the account it's decided that charges should be stopped and it's time to move forward with legal collections or write off the account. If you cannot collect the outstanding balance from the former tenant, work with your team to make a recommendation to write off the outstanding balances.

- Collect income / apply to tenants' ledgers:

You may have to apply the tenant's income as received. Hopefully the tenant is paying what was charged. If the payment is shorted do you know why? Did they miss a rent increase or an operating expense reconciliation billing? Then you may have a choice. Some areas (and you'll have to check your jurisdiction) allow a landlord to apply receipts to the oldest balances and sometimes to the oldest balances with exceptions (i.e. not to late fees). A suggestion is to apply to the charges as is indicated by the tenant. Then when you go to collections you won't be going in circles. For instance, you show rent shorted, the tenant doesn't. This is only suggested with tenants who short pay occasionally and not a habitual late payer. Each company should include a policy in their policy manual.

- Late Fees and Interest Charges:

Each lease should indicate a due date and possibly a grace period for receipt of rent. Your property database should have the ability to automatically charge late fees and interest. A LA should be aware of the local laws for applying late fees and interest. Do you have to give notice before applying either? What is the maximum interest rate allowed by law? Generally, you can't compound late fees but may be able to compound the interest and remember when charging interest for only one month the interest rate should correspond to $1/12^{th}$ of the allowed rate. If you can't set up late fees and interest charges automatically then you should calendar a reminder. Also included as a reminder are any tenants that have to have a notice before a late fee can be charged (unless your property database can automatically generate the notice).

- Work on collections and recommend charge-offs

Not usually an LA's job, but one should always be flexible – it's job security. The receivables ledger should be printed not only before applying late fees and interest but also at the end of each month. Part of the process may be balancing the account. Are there patterns of short paying (i.e. CAM increase not processed or an operating costs is in dispute)? The better information you supply to the tenant the quicker should pay (they shouldn't need as much research time). Then the LA reviews the A/R and may place a call or send a notice that the tenant has outstanding charges (and that late fees and interest may be applied). If it's not collectible a recommendation may be made to the team to charge off. Otherwise note the tenant's reason for a short pay and work under your company's policies to collect all outstanding charges. Time is of the essence the older the charges get the harder they are to collect. Can you waive late charges and interest if paid by a reasonably time (of maybe just the first time)? Can the tenant make additional payments each month to catch up on the outstanding balance?

- Review or Code Accounts Payable / Accruals:

Generally this is a property managers or accountants responsibility. Whether you code or just review you want to make sure accounts payable stays consistent. If utility bills are split to different buildings, the same split need to be made each month. Are professional fees split correctly (are they an owner's expense or a valid recoverable expense)? If you, as a LA don't already review the general ledgers you should ask to see them. If an expense is not hitting the correct expense account then the best catch is *before* the month or year is closed. This will help when you get to the end of the year and are preparing operating cost reconciliations.

If your accounting is based on accruals then each month the property manager or property accountant usually reviews the general ledger. To understand your property it is suggested that the LA also review if an expense hit on each account that should have a recurring charge? If not, an accrual, a "place marker", needs to be input. This should be set up so that once the actual expense is charged the accrual is reversed.

This is another reason to review the general ledgers is to make sure accruals are reversed, when needed, and expenses aren't overstated. You may also need to do this process for the income charges determined on whether or not the unpaid charges are collectible or not. Especially watch the taxes and insurance charges. Since they are paid in installments and usually not each month the accruals should be checked when a new billing is received and prior to processing the annual operating cost reconciliation.

If your accounting system is cash based then expenses hit when they are paid or when income is received. If your leases have Base Years and depending on your company's policies, you may have to adjust some expenses so that the annual reconciliation truly represents the annual expenses for the property. This can also be important to your leasing department for when prospective tenants ask, "What are the run rates for operating expenses for the property?"

If tenants pay their full share of operating expenses and you have a cash accounting system then it isn't as important as they will eventually pay it. However, this could depend on the company's policy or if there are any issues based on the lease language.

- Gross Sales Reports, Review Percentage
  Rent, Calculate Overages and Reports:

Gross sales are the net sales for a location,
usually retail, after exclusions to the
calculations are applied. These exclusions
(and they are different, by lease) can be
offsets for credit card fees, employee sales,
returns, online purchases, employee uniform
sales and other exclusions. Once that net
number is established then it can be
reported to the landlord. The lease may
require monthly, quarterly or annual sales
reporting. A LA then enters that information
into the property database or a Gross Sales
Report. The report should include a
calculation for sales per square foot and / or
rent to sales ratios. When compared to
national or regional databases (available
through ICSC and other groups) this can
assist the owners and teams in determining
the "health" of a tenant or property.

There are two types of Percentage Rent. The
first is when a tenant pays just a percentage
of gross sales. So the calculation is simple:
Gross Sales X Percentage Rent % = Monthly
Rent. Some landlords use this if a tenant is
struggling or some tenants include language
if the there is a lease violation (i.e.
occupancy requirements) and a tenant may
only be required to pay percentage rent
during a specific period.

The second type of percentage rent is also known as Overage Rent. When a tenant exceeds a certain amount of sales (also known as the breakpoint) then a tenant pays the percentage (as stated in the lease) in addition to rent, operating costs, etc that is already being paid by the tenant for that period of time. Please see the chapter on Percentage rent for more details.

- Budgets, Reconciliations and Challenges:

Work with your team to produce the annual operating expense budget. This can be done by the property manager, property accountant or the LA or as a team.
At the end of the year (fiscal or calendar) and after the general ledger has been reviewed and audited it's time to produce the operating expense reconciliation. For those without benefit of base years one should back into the slippage (the amount an owner pays for operating costs due to vacancy, exclusions, caps, etc.). You should be able to pin point your recovery percentage and your slippage dollars. If they don't balance then there may be an issue with your recoveries.

More information on these topics are included elsewhere in this book.

- Future impacts on the roles of the LA and the Property Accountant:

Don't be caught in the dark. Network with other Lease Administrators and Property Accountants. Ask questions – a lot of questions. Read articles on the new FASB rules or other policy updates. Take an online class or join LinkedIn. Any way you can get and understand the information is a good way. Set up and update policies, constantly. Work with your team and let the one with the strengths in a specific area (i.e. forming relationships with tenants) tackle that area.

Chapter 5
LEASE ABSTRACTION

The topics that will be discussed in this chapter will revolve around the concepts of a commercial lease document. We will be discussing what lease abstraction is and the common elements to a standard lease abstract.

To keep things into perspective, we shall go through an anatomy of a lease, typical clauses in a non-percentage rent based lease, the differences between the Commercial and Residential Tenancies Act with an emphasis on 3 key differences found within the Acts: Default/Non Payment of Rent, Hold Over and Rent. Of course there are several more differences in the acts, but we shall focus on those three. I am a resident of Ontario Canada so I will reference the Acts (Laws) as it applies here. But please note that each country, state or province will have its own laws, rules and regulations that you should follow. The information here should be considered more as a general guide

ANATOMY OF A LEASE

Let's start off this section by first defining what a commercial lease, or leasehold agreement is. A commercial lease is a written agreement between a landlord and a business tenant. This legally binding contract allows you, as the tenant, to use the commercial premises for your business activity for a specified period of time by promising to pay an agreed-upon rate to the landlord.[1]

While leasing a commercial space is often described as a two-part process, I would like to surmise that it is really a three-part process. The first step is signing an offer to lease, referred to as an OTL in the commercial field. An offer to lease is an agreement that outlines the basic business terms both parties commit to and it is from this agreement the lease is drafted. Once negotiations have taken place, the lease containing the details of the negotiations is

---

[1] http://canadabusiness.ca/eng/page/3430/

drafted. It is a wise decision to include a copy of the landlord's draft lease with the offer to lease for time-effective management and to reduce, or limit, any surprises that might arise when the formal lease is presented. This will also cut down on further negotiations and legal costs associated with signing a lease.

For purposes of stream lining the leasing process from start to finish, the third-part process would be to prepare a lease abstract upon the execution of the lease or commencement of the term. We will get to lease abstracting more later on in this chapter.

The very first difference in looking at leasing starts with the framework of the acts – what you see immediately upon first glance.

The Commercial Tenancies Act, 2006 looks something like this:

Table of Contents:
   I.   Part I
  II.   Part II
 III.   Part III

The Residential Tenancies Act, 2006 is outlined like this:

Table of Contents:

Most standard commercial leases contain a table of contents that look basically like this:

<u>Standard Commercial Lease Table of Contents:</u>

Commercial vs Residential Tenancies

The line between commercial and residential tenancies is often blurred by legislative considerations impacting both landlords and tenants (provincially). These considerations can have significant impact, as the Residential Tenancies Act affords tenants a wide range of rights not found in its commercial counterpart.[2]

While there are no government regulations, specifically for lease abstraction, there are other regulations in various sectors in real estate, such as Ontario's Commercial Tenancies Act outlining the relationship, rights and obligations between commercial landlords and tenants. It should be stated that while the Act sets out rights and obligations, the provincial government does not intervene in commercial landlord and tenant disputes.

The Residential Tenancies Act differs significantly from the Commercial Tenancies Act and the two should not be confused. In this chapter I shall show you why.

Three substantial differences between the Commercial Tenancies Act, 2006 vs The Residential Tenancies Act, R.S.O. 1990 are as follows:

I.   Rental Default/Non Payment of Rent
II. Hold Over/Overhold
III. Rent, Free Rent, Basic (Minimum) Rent, Gross Lease, Net Lease, Net Net Lease,

---

[2] The Commercial Real Estate Transaction, Real Estate Council of Ontario (RECO)

Net Net Net Lease/Triple Rent, Additional Rent, and Percentage Rent

I. Non-payment of rent is defined as the act or state of not paying[3]

Commercial

Under the Commercial Tenancies Act, R.S.O. 1990, there are two options available to landlords to cure rental default/non-payment of rent. In the example listed below, let's assume for simplicity purposes that the Tenant does not cure the default.

Option 1: Change the Locks

A landlord may change the locks of a unit and evict the tenant on the 16th day after the day rent was due. The landlord is not obligated to notify the tenant that the locks will be changed.

For example, if the rent was due on January 1st, this is how the process would look like the chart on the next page.

---

[3] The Free Dictionary, Farlex

Rent Due	Rent due on January 1st
Waiting Period	Notice of overdue rent is not required under the Act 15 days must pass before locks can be changed
Locks Changed	January 17th landlord may change the locks on unit without noficiation to the tenant

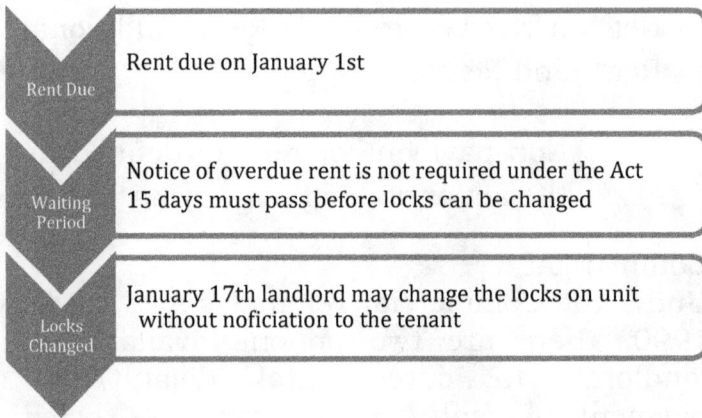

Option 2:   Seize And Dispose of Tenant's Property

A landlord may also seize and dispose of a tenant's property that is contained within the rented premises.   The landlord is not required to give advance notice of seizing the tenant's property (unless the lease provides for such notice).[4]

Residential

The remedies of rental default/ non-payment of rent fall under the Residential Tenancies Act, 2006, S.O. 2006, c. 17.   Under this legislation, there is only one option available to landlords to cure a rental default. For our purposes, let's again assume the Tenant does not cure the default.   The following

---

[4] The Commercial Real Estate Transaction, Real Estate Council of Ontario (RECO)

example outlines a monthly tenancy agreement.

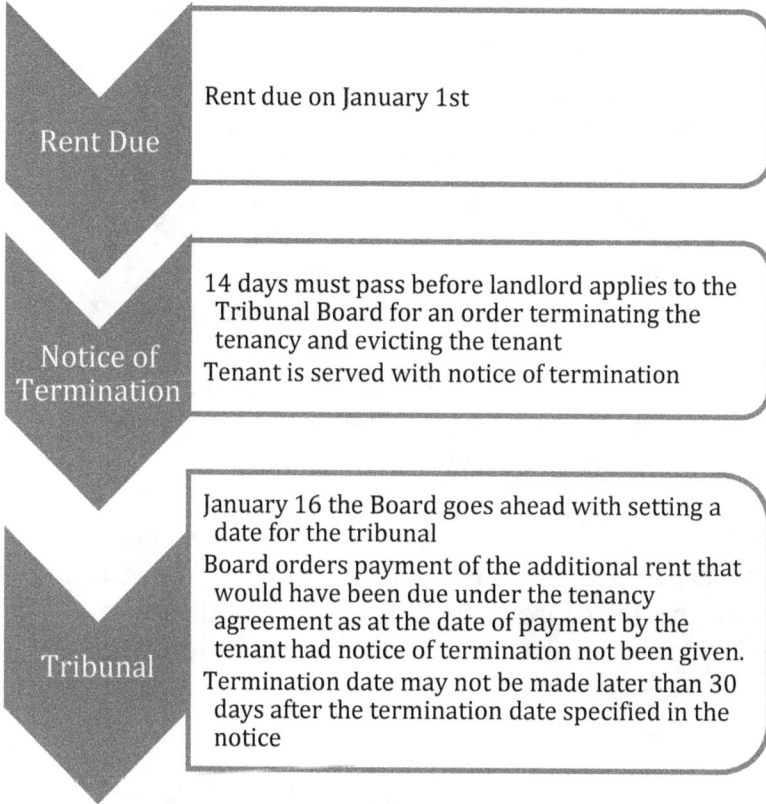

Rent Due	Rent due on January 1st
Notice of Termination	14 days must pass before landlord applies to the Tribunal Board for an order terminating the tenancy and evicting the tenant Tenant is served with notice of termination
Tribunal	January 16 the Board goes ahead with setting a date for the tribunal Board orders payment of the additional rent that would have been due under the tenancy agreement as at the date of payment by the tenant had notice of termination not been given. Termination date may not be made later than 30 days after the termination date specified in the notice

While the Commercial Tenancies Act provides for two options to cure rent default, if we look a little deeper we will see that there is in fact another option.
Option 3:

The executors or administrators of a landlord may distrain for the arrears of rent due to the landlord in the landlord's lifetime, and may sue for the same in like manner as the landlord might have done if living, and the powers and provisions contained in this Act relating to distresses for rent are applicable to the distresses so made. R.S.O. 1990, c. L.7, s. 60. [5] Distress is defined as the seizure of someone's property in order to obtain payment of rent or other money owed.[6]

The landlord may seize tenant's property or sue in order to obtain payment of money owed, more particularly rent.

To help make things a little clearer, I have created a chart for you to follow along as to what the landlord may and may not do as it pertains to both the Commercial Tenancies Act, R.S.O. 1990 and the Residential Tenancies Act S.O. 2006, C 17.

---

[5] Elaws_statutes_90l07 Commercial Tenancies Act, R.S.O. 1990, c. L.7, s. 60.

[6] https://en.wikipedia.org/wiki/Distraint

What the Landlord Can Do	What the Landlord Cannot Do
➤ Landlord can distrain for rent in commercial tenancies	➤ Landlord cannot distrain for rent in residential tenancies
➤ Landlord can distrain while the landlord and tenant relationship is in place	➤ Landlord cannot distrain after the landlord and tenant relationship has been terminated
➤ Landlord can sue for rental arrears in commercial tenancies	➤ Landlord cannot sue in the residential tenancies act, but may apply to the Board for rent so long as the overdue rent is applicable
➤ Landlord can distrain against goods or chattels (stock and inventory) belonging to the tenant in commercial tenancies	➤ Landlord cannot distrain against fixtures (an items which are physically secured to the premises) nor can the Landlord cannot distrain against goods or chattels belonging to strangers in commercial tenancies
➤ For so long as the tenant continues in possession, the landlord can distrain for rent for up to six months after the expiry of the lease in	➤ A landlord **cannot** distrain for rent after the lease has been surrendered or forfeited because the lease and the landlord-tenant relationship no longer exist. (No clause in a

commercial tenancies	lease which tries to get around this prohibition will be upheld.)
➢ Rent which is payable in advance **can** be included in the distraint provided it is deemed to be in arrears under the terms of the lease (i.e. accelerated rent which falls due upon the happening of an event) in commercial tenancies	➢ Rent which has not yet fallen due **cannot** be included in the distraint.
➢ A landlord **can** sell the goods seized by following the procedure for notice, appraisal and sale outlined in the commercial tenancies	➢ A landlord **cannot** sell the goods seized to itself, or to a non-arm's length purchaser, even at an open auction outlined in the commercial tenancies act
➢ A landlord **can** distrain before bankruptcy in commercial tenancies	➢ A landlord **cannot** distrain after the date of the bankruptcy in commercial tenancies
➢ A landlord **can** claim compensation for the cost of an incomplete distress, if the tenant becomes bankrupt in commercial tenancies	➢ A landlord **cannot** keep property or proceeds of sale from a distress which has not been completed prior to the date of bankruptcy in commercial tenancies

II.   Hold Over or Over hold is defined as the situation when a tenant of real estate continues to occupy the premises without the owner's agreement after the original lease or rental agreement between the owner (landlord) and the tenant has expired. [7]

Commercial
The Commercial Tenancies Act, R.S.O. 1990 provides for two scenarios for any hold over of the land.

Scenario 1: Penalty of double value for over holding.

Where a tenant for any term for life, lives or years, or other person who comes into possession of any land, by, from, or under, or by collusion with such tenant, willfully holds over the land or any part thereof after the determination of the term, and after notice in writing given for delivering the possession thereof by the tenant's landlord or the person to whom the remainder or reversion of the land belongs or the person's agent thereunto lawfully authorized, the tenant or other person so holding over shall, for and during the time the tenant or the

---

[7] The Free Dictionary, Farlex

other person so holds over or keeps the person entitled out of possession, pay to such person or the person's assigns at the rate of double the yearly value of the land so detained for so long as it is detained, to be recovered by action in any court of competent jurisdiction, against the recovering of which penalty there is no relief.[8]

In other words, the landlord is entitled to charge the tenant **double** its rate of rent in the last month of tenancy until either the lease is renewed or the tenant vacates the premises.

Scenario 2: Penalty of double rent for over holding after notice to quit

Where a tenant gives notice of an intention to quit the premises held by the tenant at a time mentioned in the notice and does not accordingly deliver up the possession thereof at the time mentioned in the notice, the tenant shall from thenceforward pay to the landlord double the rent or sum that the tenant should otherwise have paid, to be levied, sued for and recovered at the same times and in the same manner as the single rent or sum before the giving such notice could be levied, sued for or recovered, and

---

[8] Elaws_statutes_90l07 Commercial Tenancies Act, R.S.O. 1990, c. L.7, s. 58; 1993, c. 27, Sched.

such double rent or sum shall continue to be paid while the tenant continues in possession.[9]

Here, what it's telling you is that if a tenant gives notice to vacate the premises while in an over hold position, the rate shall also be double the value while the tenant continues to be in possession.

III.   Rent

As you can see from the diagram below, Rent has several meanings pending on the Act and even within the Act to its meaning. One must be careful when working with commercial real estate to not confuse the meanings and to correctly label the type of rent inferred.

Commercial	Residential
Free Rent is a period of time given to the landlord to occupy the space before having to commence paying rent.[10]	Rent - the amount of any consideration paid or given or required to be paid or given by or on behalf of a tenant to a landlord or the landlord's agent for the right to occupy a rental unit and for any services and

---

[9] Elaws_statutes_90l07 Commercial Tenancies Act, R.S.O. 1990, c. L.7, s. 59.
[10] Tenant Survival Institute Commercial Real Estate Dictionary

	facilities and any privilege, accommodation or thing that the landlord provides for the tenant in respect of the occupancy of the rental unit, whether or not a separate charge is made for services and facilities or for the privilege, accommodation or thing [11]
Basic Rent (sometimes referred to as Minimum Rent) can be defined as the rate at commencement of the lease. It is subject to annual increases unless otherwise negotiated in the lease or Addendum or an attached amendment.[12] Rent that a tenant pays; usually expressed as a price per square foot. Rent that is not based on a tenant's sales.[13]	
Additional Rent represents the proportionate share of operating costs, as	

---

[11] Residential Tenancies Act S.O. 2006, C 17.

[11] Tenant Survival Institute Commercial Real Estate Dictionary
[13] ICSC's Dictionary of Shopping Centre Terms, International Council of Shopping Centres

defined within the lease document. It is typically estimated at the commencement of any fiscal or calendar year for the building, with the tenant paying equal monthly installments in advance throughout the period for which the estimate is made.[14]	
Gross Lease can be defined as a lease in which the landlord pays 100 percent of all taxes, insurance, and maintenance associated with the operation of a shopping centre.[15]	
Net/Single Net Lease can be defined as a lease that is not all inclusive.[16] A lease in which the tenant agrees to pay rent and its proportionate share of the centre's ongoing expenses, such as taxes, insurance and property repairs and maintenance.[17]	

---

[14] Course 3 Advanced The Commercial Real Estate Transaction, Real Estate Counsil of Ontario (RECO)
[15] ICSC's Dictionary of Shopping Centre Terms, International Council of Shopping Centres
[16] Tenant's Survival Institute Commercial Real Estate Dictionary
[17] ICSC's Dictionary of Shopping Centre Terms, International

Net Net Lease can be defined as a lease in which the tenant pays maintenance and operating expenses, plus property taxes. However, this usually excludes structural repairs to the external structure.[18]	
Net Net Net/Triple Net Lease can be defined as a lease in which 100 percent of all taxes, insurance; and maintenance associated with a property is paid by the tenant.[19]	
Percentage Rent can be defined as a percentage of the tenant's total annual sales paid in addition to fixed rent. Extra rent paid to a landlord if a tenant's sales figures exceed a prearranged figure.[20]	

Council of Shopping Centres
[18] The Commercial Real Estate Transaction, Real Estate Council of Ontario (RECO)
[19] ICSC's Dictionary of Shopping Centre Terms, International Council of Shopping Centres
[20] ICSC's Dictionary of Shopping Centre Terms, International Council of Shopping Centres

Lease Abstraction

What exactly is a lease abstract? Simply put, a lease abstract is a summary of specific financial, business and legal information from a lengthy lease document that allows the users to locate frequently referenced fundamental items in the lease without needing to continually go through the entire document. The abstract acts as a condensation of the original lease document. It brings to the reader's attention any unusual lease provisions, financial obligations, important dates or other issues of importance and shows the reader where to look for further information in the lease. **The key to a valuable lease abstract is to keep things short and simple.**

The common person is not meant to understand the terminology and legalese contained within a lease. Taking the guess work out of leasing space gives a clear picture of what both landlord and tenant are signing. Thousands of dollars can be saved by fully comprehending what they are signing. For tenants, key items they would want brought to their attention might include wanting to find out if, and under what conditions, they may have in breaking a lease, costs associated with buying vs leasing commercial property, any renewal options and notice dates, step ups in the rent, operating expenses....the list goes on. For landlords, their focal points of attention would be drawn to renewal options and notice dates as well, but also restrictive covenants, radius clauses, repair and maintenance, tenant's insurance and so forth.

In addition to a lease abstract, there is also a something called a lease summary, not to be confused with a lease abstract. A lease summary is a simplified version of an abstract - an abstract traditionally can consist of technical language pending on the end user while the summary contains non-technical language. A summary is typically used for tenants and leasing agents as opposed to investors or facility management companies.

Benefits of a Lease Abstract

Commercial leases are usually abstracted to assist in locating frequently referenced items in the lease without needing to continually go through the entire document. Commercial leases usually include a large degree of legal language that can make it difficult to quickly find critical lease data.

Additionally, all of the financial terms of the lease deal are documented in the abstract, which makes it useful for property investors or lenders. Providing a lease abstract rather than a full lease text saves time and money for those who are performing due diligence on the property for a potential sale or acquisition.

Who should have a Lease Abstracted?

- Facility Management Companies
- Investors/Buyers
- Landlords
- Lease Administrators
- Leasing Agent
- Lenders
- Maintenance Workers
- Property Managers
- Tenants
- Trustees in Bankruptcy
- Realtors/Brokers
- Anyone involved with commercial real estate

As we can see from the list above, literally anyone involved in commercial real estate benefits from having a lease abstracted. The top four which I have identified are listed here, with the why behind it.

Investors	Lease review is critical to the acquisition process for publicly held real estate investment trusts (REITS), and privately held real estate investing companies as well as for individual investors. Leases should also be abstracted when a property changes management.
Lenders	Reviewing tenant leases and analyzing projected future income are essential due diligence tasks for underwriters and investment banks.
Property Managers	Effective day-to-day management of any property ultimately depends upon a thorough understanding of its lease documentation.
Tenants	Tenants often compile numerous leases over time and require abstracting services in order to track and audit critical lease data.

Why is a Lease Abstract Needed?

Lease abstracting becomes particularly important prior to an acquisition, merger or assignment of a lease and allows for effective decision-making. It provides bottom line information extracted by experts after careful consideration and integration of all relevant documents. Abstracts also permit a lease administrator, leasing agent or property manager to easily review all relevant lease information without taking the time to search and read through each page of the lease. By collecting the lease information, abstracts allow users to better manage a portfolio of leases. Lease abstracting serves to organize your lease data, which is a crucial benefit when leases contain many amendments, when landlords or tenants hold sizeable lease assets, or when dealing with a variety of lease formats.

What Lease Information Should be Abstracted:

The lease information that should be abstracted depends on the individual needs of the client and is contingent on several factors, including the reasons for abstracting and the length and complexity of the lease document. Lease abstracts can range anywhere from two to ten pages, but typically consist of three to five pages. At a minimum, an abstract should contain the most important "dates and dollars" provisions of the lease, such as the commencement date, expiration of the term, any renewal terms and other key options along with rents, operating expenses, and square footages.

Why Do We Need a Lease Abstract Anyways?

The lease is critical to those involved with commercial real estate. Landlords and tenants have rights and obligations and the lease sets out the particulars of those rights and obligations.

Types of Lease Abstracts:

I. Basic
II. Standard
III. Comprehensive
IV. Parking
V. Storage
VI. Amendments or Renewals
VII. Tower
VIII. Kiosk

What Is Abstracted?
The diagram on the next page gives you a general picture of the hierarchy outline to a lease abstracted. What precisely is abstracted is contingent upon the goal or purpose of the abstract.

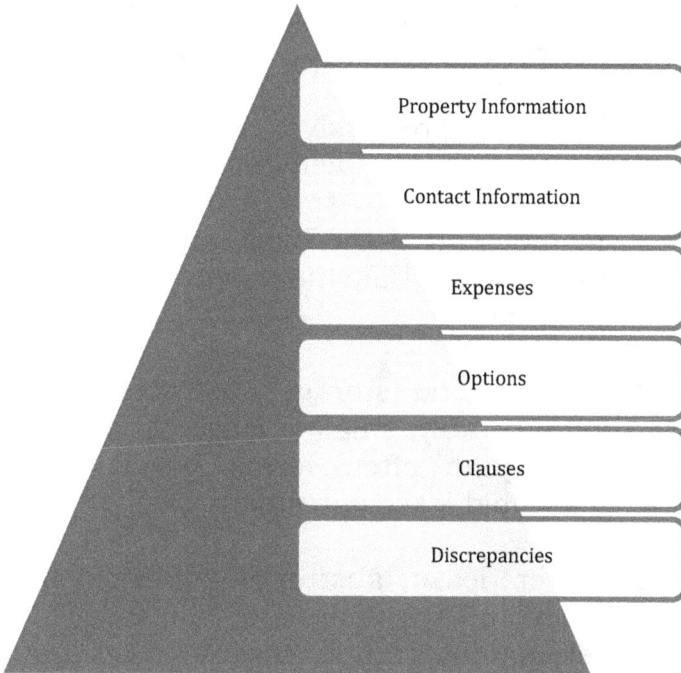

Below I have outlined a definition of each type of abstract listed above. By no means are the descriptions exhaustive, it merely captures the essence of the abstract.

1. The basic lease abstract provides a general picture of the lease while summarizing dates and dollars in greater detail.

2. The standard lease abstract provides a snapshot of the most commonly referenced lease provisions. It includes all of the basic abstract

identification, plus additional information.

3. The comprehensive lease abstract provides a complete summary of all the salient lease provisions. It includes all of the basic and standard abstract identification, plus additional information.

4. Parking and storage abstracts are a considerably smaller lease document, and quite often forms part of the leasehold lease agreement.

5. Tower lease abstracts provides the rules and regulations of "air space" to telecommunication towers. Yes you read that correctly, air space. While this sort of lease agreement relates to only telecommunication systems, it is still vitally important to have abstracted, perhaps even more so due to the relative ease in which theft can occur.

6. And like the names suggest, lease amendments and renewals are extensions of the original lease document. These sorts of abstracts are woven into the original lease abstract noting any changes of pre-

existing terms, dates or dollars any cancellations thereof.

TENANTS

I wanted to include a section that focuses directly with tenants as without them, there would be no commercial real estate as the need for it would not exist. Because the Commercial Tenancies Act is landlord biased, I wanted to put some control back into the hands of the tenants and not feel as there are no options for them out there. There is. Tenants just need the right tools and people on their team.

The first-time tenant often wants to complete most of the work by him or herself to save costs, however in an effort to save costs the Tenant inadvertently compromises him or herself financially and may very well risk the success or survival of the business. The first-time tenant frequently:

- Experiences considerable difficulty in locating and obtaining a suitable location;
- Lacks contacts and are limited in their available free-time to research locations;
- Does not appreciate the many and variable costs that will be incurred;

- Fails to understand that rental costs can vary dramatically, even among similar properties;
- Faces stringent credit/experience checks;
- Fails to realize that special facilities may not be readily available or economically viable for their particular operation, or what facilities are needed (cook-stove vent, fire-control services, special security systems)
- Underestimates the high cost of fixtures and stocking, and associated cost of capital to open the operation;
- Fails to understand the contents of a Lease.

The first-time tenant often wants to complete most of the finishing work by him or herself to save costs, however the Landlord frowns on this approach as complications can arise (i.e. failure to meet standards and liability issues). Sometimes the Landlord may agree to a tenant's allowance that must be applied to improvements.

The owner of a commercial property is interested in maximizing cash flow, procuring an adequate return on investment and obtaining the most appealing grouping (tenant mix) of diverse uses geared to a particular market . The first-time tenant is an important ingredient in any structured mix, along with multi-use or major tenants.

Tenants, while hunting for that perfect location for your business, it's a good idea to go with a shopping list, much like shopping with a grocery list, to keep in the forefront what your basic needs are. I have given you a head start here to simplify the task as much as possible.

<u>Shopping Checklist</u>
- Decide what things you want to have included in your lease. Divide those items into non-negotiable and nice-to-have items to help you stay firm on and what you can compromise on.
- Determine the length of time of the term.
- Determine the location – are you a destination service or need high visibility to draw in traffic?
- Determine what you can afford to pay monthly, all costs inclusive.
- Shop around to find out what insurance is going to cost you and if you need any forms of insurance due to machinery, fumes, glass, etc.
- Look at your competition. How far are they from you? Is there a similar service in the location area?

- Determine if exclusivity is important to you or an imposed radius clause by a landlord.
- Solicitor fees obligations in the event of disagreements – or better yet, abstraction services to avoid those disagreements.
- Check with city by-laws for signage requirements if signage is important to you.
- Decide if you want to rent a vanilla shell box and fixture according to your needs. If so determine costs ahead of time so you know what you will be paying. Or do you prefer taking over an existing service with all fixtures included?
- Utility obligations – yours or the landlords?
- Shape of the building – is it falling apart or in relatively decent condition?
- Decide on what tenant mix would benefit you.
- Decide on what tenant mix would not benefit you.
- Are you a first time tenant? Have a guarantor or indemnifier name on hand just in case the landlord requires one.

- Make sure you have sufficient security deposit on hand.

If after reading this chapter you are still unsure about abstracting your lease, keep in mind that there is a cost to not knowing....the price you could pay down the road could be too high.

Chapter 6
DIFFERENT TYPES OF LEASES AND RENT STRUCTURES

(Gross Lease, Net Lease, Modified Gross Lease)

In Commercial Real Estate, there are three basic types and leases are organized around two rent calculation methods: "net" and "gross." The gross lease means a tenant pays one lump sum for rent, from which the landlord pays his expenses. The net lease has a smaller base rent, with other expenses paid for by the tenant. The modified gross lease is similar to a gross lease in that the rent is requested in one lump sum, which can include any or all of the "nets"--property taxes, insurance, and CAMS. The below chapter defines the different types of leases and rent structures.

Different Types of Leases and Rent Structures:
In Commercial Real Estate, there are three basic types and leases are organized around

two rent calculation methods: "net" and "gross."
1. Gross Lease or Full Service Lease
2. Net Lease
3. Modified Gross Lease

1. Gross Lease or Full Service Lease:
The gross lease means a tenant pays one lump sum for rent, from which the landlord pays his expenses. In a gross lease, the rent is all-inclusive. The landlord pays all or most expenses associated with the property, including taxes, insurance, and maintenance out of the rents received from tenants. Utilities and janitorial services are included within one easy, tenant-friendly rent payment.

2. Net Lease:
In a net lease, the landlord charges a lower base rent for the commercial space, plus some or all of "usual costs," which are expenses associated with operations, maintenance, and use that the landlord pays. These can include real estate taxes; property insurance; and common area maintenance items (CAMS), which include janitorial services, property management fees, sewer, water, trash collection, landscaping, parking lots, fire sprinklers, and any commonly shared area or service.

Different Types of Net Leases:
Single Net Lease (N Lease):
In this lease, the tenant pays base rent plus a pro-rata share of the building's property tax; the landlord covers all other building expenses. The tenant also pays utilities and janitorial services.

Double Net Lease (NN Lease):
The tenant is responsible for base rent plus a pro-rata share of property taxes and property insurance. The landlord covers expenses for structural repairs and common area maintenance. The tenant once again is responsible for their own janitorial and utility expenses.

Triple Net Lease (NNN Lease):
This is the most popular type of net lease for commercial freestanding buildings and retail space. It is known as the net net net lease, or NNN lease, where the tenant pays all or part of the three "nets"--property taxes, insurance, and CAMS--on top of a base monthly rent. Common area utilities and operating expenses are usually lumped in as well; for example, the cost for staffing a lobby attendant would be part of the NNN fees. Of course, tenants also pay the costs of their own occupancy, including janitorial services, utilities, and their own insurance and taxes.

Triple net leases tend to be more landlord-friendly, and tenants should carefully review NNN fees and negotiate caps on the amounts they can be raised annually.

Absolute Triple Net Lease:
This is a less common option that is more rigid and binding than the NNN lease, where tenants carry every imaginable real estate risk, for example, being responsible for construction expenses to rebuild after a catastrophe or for continuing to pay rent even after the building has been condemned. Aptly called the "hell-or-high-water lease," tenants have ultimate responsibility for the building no matter what.

Modified Gross Lease:
The modified gross lease is similar to a gross lease in that the rent is requested in one lump sum, which can include any or all of the "nets"--property taxes, insurance, and CAMS. Utilities and janitorial services are typically excluded from the rent, and covered by the tenant. Tenants and landlords negotiate which "nets" are included in the base rental rate.

Summary

In Commercial Real Estate, there are three basic types and leases are organized around two rent calculation methods: "net" and "gross." The gross lease means a tenant pays one lump sum for rent, from which the landlord pays his expenses. The net lease has a smaller base rent, with other expenses paid for by the tenant. The modified gross lease is similar to a gross lease in that the rent is requested in one lump sum, which can include any or all of the "nets"--property taxes, insurance, and CAMS. The below chapter defines the different types of leases and rent structures. As the gross lease is more tenant-friendly, and the net lease tends to be more landlord-friendly, there exists a compromise lease for the convenience of both parties. The modified gross lease is a happy marriage between the two.

Chapter 7
ABOUT THE
OFFER TO LEASE

There is so much one can write about the offer to lease agreement. You can write about the process leading up to the offer to lease, the content of the offer to lease, the negotiations, the due diligence during the conditional period and many other things. The following information provides you with a snapshot of some of the language and items that are important in an offer to lease from my perspective and experience. There is certainly a lot more insight to an offer to lease then what I have written, but I think the following will provide some knowledge along with some great advice and a good basis to understand the offer to lease.

Over the years tenants, landlords and brokers have become much more knowledgeable and this knowledge has generally been gained through several bad experiences during the offer to lease stage.

A tenant may have been burned by vague operating cost language. A landlord may have been extremely eager to obtain a national tenant with an excellent covenant be part of their portfolio that they oversaw some of the exclusivities granted as not being relevant at the time. A broker may have told their client what they wanted to hear only to lose their biggest client as a result of it. As a result of bad experiences and also some good experiences along the way, I think the drafting of an offer to lease has changed tremendously over the past two decades. Most sophisticated landlords, tenants and several brokerage firms have their own standard offer to lease form, which they prefer to use. When you are not using your own standard form of lease, your chances of not seeing specific language relating to something important to you can easily missed. It is extremely important to be detailed oriented and take the time necessary to review the agreement and compare the offer to lease form to your standard form. You will be surprised to see where language has been buried in the offer to lease.

Guidelines to drafting an offer to lease

From my experience and prospective drafting an offer to lease is a form of art. Some people have a natural way with words and others must labour at it more. Regardless of your writing skills, you must become an effective drafter of basic terms and an interpreter of your standard offer to lease and other parties' documents. The good thing is that leasing is largely standardized which allows the drafter to develop and enhance their drafting skills over a period of time. Practice, more practice and experience are critical to the drafter becoming an expert.

The offer to lease reflects what the tenant and landlord have negotiated, agreed to, and bound by. While the offer to lease is a much standard form then the lease agreement, it should be detailed, and its provisions should not be subject to multiple interpretations. The basic business terms and conditions in the offer to lease should be considered final with perhaps minor revisions within reason - so long as it does not materially affect the business provisions and terms.

The approach to leasing space is for the landlord and tenant to negotiate the basic terms and conditions of the lease, and incorporate these into a binding offer to lease agreement. The reason for this two-step process, first the offer and then the lease is as follows:

- The offer to lease, if detailed, will accurately state all of the key terms and conditions the parties have negotiated and agreed to.
- The offer to lease is generally about 15% to 30% of the size of the Landlord's or Tenant's master lease template. It therefore expedites the process.
- The offer to lease is fully binding, so the Landlord can begin the process of tendering the tenant improvements and planning for the tenant's occupancy. The tenant can now prepare for their new premises, including advising all other relevant parties of their new business location.
- The offer to lease is subservient to the master lease template. This allows the tenant and the landlord the necessary time to work on the final wording of the lease which normally takes approximately two to four weeks.

- An offer to lease usually contains the following provisions:

a) description of the premises (building address, suite, floor square feet, type of measurement);
b) term (period for which the tenant and landlord are leasing the space, example; five (5) years commencing on July 1, 2015 and expiring on June 30, 2018);
c) rent (net rent, semi – gross rent, gross rent);
d) additional rent (if the offer is a net or semi gross);
e) security deposit;
f) use;
g) free rent;
h) renewal or extension periods;
i) fixturing period;
j) landlord's work;
k) tenant's work;
l) parking;
m) signage;
n) equipment;
o) tenant allowance or tenant inducement;

p) irrevocable date;

q) notice;

r) time of the essence;

s) indemnity agreement;

t) time for acceptance (for both landlord and tenant);

u) entire agreement, binding language;

v) material clauses to the parties such as relocation and demolition;

w) concessions provided by landlord to the tenant, such as right of first offer, right of first refusal, termination option; and

x) other provisions and schedules depending on the terms and conditions of the offer to lease.

It's quite fine to take months to negotiate an offer to lease, always keep in mind that the terms and conditions may be in effect for years. It's critical to understand and know what you want to achieve, and what your parameters are, before you commence negotiations. Have an objective and realistic leasing game plan, and the discipline to adhere to it. Use the time during negotiations to secure as many advantageous concessions as possible, verify and conclude any outstanding issues, one by one as much as the final lease form and content as possible during the offer to lease negotiations.

In the past it was acceptable to both parties if material provisions in the offer to lease weren't explicit and extremely detailed – little "broad" was acceptable. The understanding was, the provision would be sorted out at the lease agreement stage. Currently tenants are becoming more educated and learning from "'bad experiences." For example, a relocation clause in the offer to lease may be written as follows: *"The Landlord may have the right to relocate the tenant during the term of the lease."* In the lease agreement it will be written as follows: *"The Landlord shall have the right from time to time, on not less than sixty (60) days' notice to the Tenant, to relocate the Premises to other premises within the Building having approximately the same area as the Premises. If the Landlord relocates the Premises prior to occupancy by the Tenant, it shall reimburse the Tenant for all reasonable out-of-pocket expenses already incurred by the Tenant in preparing to move into the Premises to the extent that such expenditure is for items or materials not usable in the alternate premises. If the Landlord relocates the Tenant after occupancy by the Tenant, the Landlord shall provide the relocated premises improved to a standard and using materials of approximately the same quality as the leasehold improvements which exist in the existing Premises at the time of relocation and reimburse the Tenant (upon receipt of copies of receipted third party invoices) for direct costs associated with the relocation, including, without limitation, moving costs, reprinting of a limited supply of stationery and supplies and disconnection and reconnection of telephone and computer equipment and systems. In no case will the Tenant be reimbursed or compensated for indirect costs including overhead, overtime charges or loss of profits and the Tenant will minimize costs by re-using all fixtures and trade fixtures from the Premises where it is feasible to do so. The Landlord agrees to use reasonable efforts to effect the relocation with a minimum of disruption to the Tenant's business. The Landlord and the Tenant shall enter into a lease amending agreement in the Landlord's standard form to confirm the terms of the relocation including, without limitation, any adjustment to the Rent if the rentable area of the relocated premises is different than the Rentable Area of the Premises and to confirm that all other terms and conditions of this Lease shall apply with respect to the relocated premises for the remainder of the Term."* The tenant may argue at the lease stage lease that the relocation clause was not written this way in the offer and the language will not be accepted. This will cause unnecessary debate. In the end the landlord and tenant may not be able to agree. One of the parties will be at risk of losing a major item that is extremely critical to their business.

Another example is "demolition." The offer may be written as follows, *"The Landlord has the right to terminate the Lease at any time." In the lease the demolition clause may read as follows, "If the Landlord intends to demolish or substantially renovate the whole or a major part of the Building which requires vacant possession of the Premises, the Landlord may terminate this Lease by giving at least six (6) months prior written notice to the Tenant. In such event, the Tenant shall vacate the Premises in the manner contemplated herein on or before the date set out in such notice."* Again this may be an issue as the detail was not agreed to in the offer and one of the parties could be comprising their business.

The important thing to remember for both landlord and tenant is to negotiate the clauses in detail at the offer stage if they are of extreme importance and value. This rule applies to all material clauses. Remember if it's important to have items occur during a certain period, in certain way it's important to be clear and detailed.

If for any reason a clause cannot be written in a detailed manner in the offer, the clause should end in *"as further detailed in the lease."* For example, *"The landlord shall have the right to relocate the tenant as set out in more detailed in the lease."* In this case the lease should be attached to the offer as a schedule.

If the lease is being attached to the offer make sure the offer contains a clause that is clear such as the lease shall incorporate the terms and conditions of the offer in the landlord's standard form of lease or the terms and conditions and of the lease will be incorporated in the lease with revisions made to the lease.

An example of the both clauses are below:

"The Tenant agrees to execute the Landlord's standard form of lease, a copy of which is attached hereto as Schedule A, which shall incorporate the provisions set out in this Offer

to Lease, within thirty (30) days from the date hereof."

OR

"The Landlord's standard form of lease, a copy of which is attached hereto as Schedule "A" is subject to reasonable negotiations, provided that if the form of lease is not settled and signed by both parties within thirty (30) days from the date hereof of this agreement shall be null and void and the tenant's deposit shall be returned to it forwith without deduction or interest."

Five Elements of a Contract

The offer to lease should always include the five elements of a contract, which are;

1) Parties Intent to create a legal relation
2) Meeting of the minds (offer and acceptance)
3) Exchange of value (consideration)
4) Parties must have the capacity to enter into a contract
5) Lawful purpose

These elements of contract make the offer to lease a binding contract which is important so that the Landlord and tenant can prepare the tenant for move in.

There are certainly many elements one can write about an offer to lease, but hopefully this short section can provide you with a sense for how critical the offer to lease is. It is the agreement that may govern the legal relationship between the tenant and landlord should a lease never be signed. Ensure your offer to lease is sufficient to govern the relationship if the lease is not signed.

Chapter 8
LEASE COMMENCEMENT PROVISIONS
Is This The Start Of Something Great?

Lease Commencement; it's when the lease and obligation to pay rents starts, right? Not........! How can a simple, innocuous provision be so confusing and complicated? By my unofficial guess, over half of the lease issues that I've dealt with, over the last 39 years, have involved disputes over when the lease commenced and when the party's obligations started and ended.

The problem with the typical commencement language in commercial leases is just that; nothing is typical except that nothing is typical. As compared to residential leases, nearly everything is negotiable in a commercial lease and what one party gives to the other, in one provision, they may take away in another.

Let me take this opportunity to confuse you:

- First, the lease date is not necessarily and is often, not the commencement date of the lease.

- Second, the lease commencement date is not necessarily when the tenant is obligated to start paying rent.......... or building operating expenses............... or CAM charges.............. or provide insurance, etc.

- Third, neither the date of the lease nor the lease commencement date are necessarily the date that the tenant receives the keys to the space and can take possession of the premises.

Now, let's step back a bit and try to define a few things:

The "Date of the Lease" or "Lease Date" is usually used for the sole purpose of helping identify the lease document and is often stated in the first paragraph of the lease. It is intended to distinguish the lease document from other documents or agreements between the landlord and tenant, including later amendments to the lease and various other versons. Typical lease date language includes:

1. *"The date of this lease is July 4, 2015, by and between.........."; or*

2. *"For reference purposes, the date of this lease is July 4, 2015.........."; or*
3. *"The effective date of the lease is July 4, 2015, notwithstanding the date that the lease is signed"; or*
4. *"This lease is dated, for reference purposes, the last date that this lease is signed by the landlord and tenant."*

For the purpose of clarity, I prefer the third example because it is the clearest expression of the date of the lease, for identification purposes. Keep in mind that we are just trying to identify the document for later reference. I disfavor the fourth example because it forces the parties to reference another portion of the lease document which opens the door to later confusion or misinterpretation.

The "Lease Commencement" date is often, but not necessarily, used as a date that triggers other events and obligations of the landlord or tenant, including:

- When the tenant gets the keys and has the right to take possession;
- When the tenant must start paying rents, including CAM

charges, building operating expenses;
- When rent escalations take affect;
- When the tenant must provide insurance covering its business and the premises;
- When the tenant must communicate its intention to exercise an option to extend the lease beyond the original term; and
- when the lease term ends.

In many instances, the landlord, as part of the lease, will agree to delay the tenant's obligation to make payments required by the lease. This is often expressed by the following examples:

1. The effective date of the lease is July 4th;
   1.1.   The lease commences August 1, 2015, but the tenant's obligation to pay rent does not commence until October 1, 2015; or
   1.2.   The lease and rent commencement date is August 1, 2015, but the landlord agrees to forgive or *"conditionally forgive"*[21] rent

___

[21] When the landlord forgives rent without any conditions, the tenant's obligation to pay rent for the specified period of time is, permanently discharged. A conditional forgiveness of rent

for the months of August and September 2015; or

1.3.   The lease commences October 1, 2015, but the landlord will allow "early possession" to the tenant on August 1, 2015. It is typically stated that the tenant is allowed early possession in order to do its construction and tenant improvements, although there need not be any reason or reason stated.

Each of the above examples, seemingly have the same effect and results, which couldn't be further from the truth. In all three examples, the tenant's obligation to start paying monthly rent starts on October 1st. Assume for these examples, that the initial term of the lease is 5 years or 60 months. Without further clarification, the lease in examples 1.1 and 1.2 would terminate on July 31, 2020. However, in example 1.3, the lease would terminate on September 30, 2020. In examples 1.1 and 1.2, the landlord should receive and the tenant should pay rent for 58 months. In example 1.3, the tenant should be paying rent for a full 60 months.

---

usually allows the landlord to "claw back" the free rent in the event the tenant later defaults. In essence, the landlord is stating that he is offering the discount of the free rent upon the condition that the tenant fully performs its obligations for the full term of the lease.

In instances where the landlord wants payment for the full 60 months or where the landlord wants or needs to have the lease terminate on a specific date[22], the lease term in examples 1.1 and 1.2 can be increased to 62 months, thus extending the term of the lease through September 30, 2015.

If I haven't confused you yet, don't worry, I will. The key takeaways from examples 1.1 – 1.3 is that the landlord and tenant have competing interests and that the more they modify the lease terms to satisfy their own interests, the greater the opportunity for confusion and mistakes.

Since we are discussing the difference between the lease commencement date and the rent commencement date, early possession and free rent, I suppose we should clarify what we mean by rent. Rent can mean a lot of different things and should be clearly defined in the lease.

---

[22] In situations in which the landlord has subdivided larger spaces into smaller, individual rentals to accommodate smaller tenants, the landlords should have all of the leases for the subdivided space, terminate on the same date in order to give the landlord the option, at the end of the lease terms to lease the combined, undivided space to a larger occupant, if it is to the landlord's advantage

I can't, in this chapter, go into a full description of the various, permutations and meanings of the term rent, which will be explained in more detail in this book, for the purpose of this chapter, we will assume that rent means monthly base rent or minimum monthly rents, excluding any other payment obligations of the tenant, including CAM charges, building operating expenses, taxes, insurance, reimbursement for capital improvements, etc. These payment obligations of the tenant, other than base rent, I will refer to as "Additional Rent", which is a term often used in leases to distinguish these payment obligations of the tenant from base rent or minimum monthly rent.

The distinction between "rent" and "Additional Rent" is very important and often misunderstood when the lease provides that the lease commencement date is different from the rent commencement date or when the landlord offers free rent or early possession. When the lease commencement date differs from the rent commencement date, the lease must clearly state whether or not the date the tenant must start paying rent, includes the obligation to pay additional rent. While it is true that most leases include the definitions of the terms, "rent", "base rent", "minimum monthly rent", "additional rent" or other similar terms later in the lease, if there is a "rent commencement clause" separate and apart from the lease commencement clause, I prefer to include the following optional provisions:

In instances in which the tenant has no obligation to pay anything prior to the rent commencement date:

> *"All monthly obligations to make payments to the landlord as provided for in this lease, whether considered base rent, monthly minimum rent, additional rent, CAM charges, building operating expenses or similar payment obligations, commence on August 1, 2015"* or

In instances in which the tenant is not obligated to pay "base rent" or the "minimum monthly rent" at the time of possession or for a set period of time after the lease commencement date:

> *"Notwithstanding anything else contained herein to the contrary, with the exception of base rent or the minimum monthly rent payments required in this lease, all obligations to pay additional rent, CAM charges, building*

operating expenses or similar payment obligations, commence on August 1, 2015"

Even when landlords allow free rents or early possession, it is not uncommon to require the tenant to pay additional rent during the period of time that the tenant is in possession but not paying base rent. From the landlord's perspective the payment of additional rent is a reimbursement of the landlord's expenses.

While we are on the subject of free rent or early possession, I strongly recommend that landlord's require the tenant to provide insurance coverage as required by the lease at all times that the tenant has the legal right to possession of the premises

Let's now tackle one additional issue that often arises when the landlord is not sure when it can deliver possession of the premises. What if, at the time that the lease is executed, the landlord and tenant are not sure when the lease will commence? This issue typically arises when:

1. The property upon and/or the building within which the premises will be located

is not yet constructed at the time of lease execution;

2. The landlord has not yet obtained possession of the premises from an existing tenant with an expiring lease; or

3. The landlord is obligated to do some construction in the premises and deliver the premises to the tenant in an agreed upon condition. The agreed upon condition may be:

   • The completion of the exterior walls, floors and ceiling as well as bringing the utilities to the premises, leaving all internal construction and tenant improvements the responsibility of the tenant, (typical in retail and industrial leases); or

   • Turn-key, move-in condition, with all internal walls, ceilings doors, HVAC, operational and perhaps wall covering and flooring completed, typical in office leases.

The issues that can arise in instances in which the commencement date is not determined until some time after the lease is executed, are too numerous to thoroughly discuss in this chapter. However, some of the typical issues that arise are:

   • Once the parties have agreed upon the commencement date, they fail to memorialize the date in a writing such as a letter;

- Unforeseen circumstances are more the rule than the exception. Existing tenants don't move out timely, and construction is always delayed. When you have a deadline, count on it. Careful parties will negotiate a "drop-dead" date in the lease that allows one or both parties to cancel the lease if the landlord does not or cannot deliver possession by that date.

- In instances where the landlord is required to do the tenant improvements and deliver the premises with the improvements completed, attached to the lease is usually, a "work-letter" that specifies the work to be done by the landlord and the timing of all matters relating to the construction. Typically, the landlord will notify the tenant when construction is completed and the date that the landlord will be delivering the premises to the tenant, allowing the landlord and tenant sufficient time and opportunity to inspect the premises and note whatever corrections and issues remain relating to the construction and condition of the premises. In these circumstances, it is usually required by the lease and good business practice to document the inspection and any "punch-list" items that need correction as well as document the commencement date.

Rather than step back a moment, let's move forward to later lease events that can be affected by the lease commencement date, namely the lease termination date and any options to extend the term of the lease.

The lease termination date is often calculated taking into consideration, the lease commencement date and adding the number of months in the term of the lease. This is not rocket science. You would not believe how many times I have seen leases where the commencement date is clearly stated, the term of the lease is clear, but the termination date is calculated incorrectly. The example below is a common error.

"Lease commencement is April 1, 2005
Term of the lease is 3 years
The lease term ends April 30 2008"

In an effort to clearly define the termination date, the drafters of the lease make a common drafting error by miscalculating the term of the lease. If the third line of this example is controlling, then the lease term is actually 3 years and one month or 37 months. If the second line of this example is controlling, then the lease term ends on March 31st, not April 30th.

You may ask, why is the lease termination date significant?

First, unless provided otherwise in the lease, the tenant has no legal right to remain in possession of the lease beyond the lease termination date and the landlord can proceed to evict the tenant.

Second, many leases have holdover provisions stating that in the event the tenant holds over and remains in possession of the premises beyond the term of the lease, the rent owed by the tenant for the period that they remain in possession beyond the termination date is increased by a multiple of the rents owed during the last month of the lease term. I have seen that multiple being as high as three times the last months rent, an obligation that is usually, somewhat onerous for the tenant.

Third, and this is an issue that I see most often, a dispute arises as to whether or not the tenant properly and timely exercised its option to extend the term of the lease.

As part of the initial lease negotiations, tenants often seek an option to extend the term of the lease, beyond the initial term. An option to extend the term of the lease for a set period of time is rarely to the landlord's benefit, but often agreed to by the landlord. Although usually agreeing to an option, landlords often protect themselves by restricting the time period within which the tenant can give notice of its intent to exercise the option. This time period is usually calculated backwards from the termination date of the lease. An example of a common timing provision in an option clause of a lease is:

> *"Tenant may exercise the option to extend the term of the lease an additional five years, by delivering written notice to the landlord, no sooner than 6 months prior to the end of the term of the lease and no later than 3 months prior to the end of the term of the lease, evidencing its intent to exercise the option, no sooner than 6 months prior to the end of the term of the lease and no later than 3 months prior to the end of the term of the lease."*

If the commencement date is unclear and the corresponding termination date is unclear, there is an excellent chance that the tenant may miss this very narrow window to exercise its option is significant. I have litigated this issue, at least a half a dozen times. In many cases, the option is a very valuable right and asset that the tenant has negotiated. The failure to timely exercise the option can be a very costly mistake for the tenant.

In this chapter, we have touched upon, only a few of the many issues that may arise relating to the commencement clauses of a commercial lease. If there is one concept that you should take away from this discussion is that a negotiating and drafting a commercial real estate lease is not an easy process and Clarity is good, volume is not. Attorneys focus their efforts drafting a document that clearly states the intent of the landlord and tenant. Clarity often requires greater specificity, which in turn often complicates the lease further.

Chapter 9
FIVE LANDLORD RELATED INCOME POOLS

In another chapter, we will discuss recoveries. "Recoveries" is a general term relating to the landlord recovering the operating costs of the property, of which there are many. Prior to that discussion it is important to understand how the landlord receives income.

If you look at the price of something in a store such as an item of food, a car or clothing you will see one price. Conversely, the lease contains various separate types of income to the landlord.

Imagine if the storeowner posted a break down of the costs that went into the item and multiple prices on their price tag for items such as material, rent, shipping, labour, shrinkage, administration and profit (to name a few). The reason the storeowner doesn't do this is because the inventory turns quickly so it is easy to adjust the price of the product as market conditions change.

Conversely, a lease is over a long period of time and many variables come into play. As a result, the commercial real estate industry has evolved a system in most leases that pool various types of income for the landlord, or expense for the tenant depending on your point of view. Here is an overview of the five general categories. They are: minimum rent, percentage rent (in retail properties), common area recoveries, property tax recovery and tenant specific recoveries.

Minimum Rent
This also goes by several other names such as basic rent and base rent. This is the rent the tenant pays to occupy the space or obtain rights to use the space and includes air-rights, ground rent, etc.

This rent covers the **expenses personal to the landlord**, including mortgage costs, costs to generate income, such as leasing commissions or salaries, leasehold improvements, the landlord's income taxes, etc. The landlord's profit margin is also included in the minimum rent.

Minimum rent tends to be fairly stable over the term simply because there is low volatility of the costs the landlord must pay out of the minimum rent it collects. For example, mortgages tend to be over periods of time that can stretch many years so the landlord's mortgage cost is predictable for a long time.

Percentage Rent

Again, different people call this by different names that include percent rent, overage rent, sales rent, etc. This type of rent is only found in certain retail properties as it is tied to the sales of the tenant. Skeptics often refer to this rent as the Landlord's Mistake Rent as a result.

We take a different view of percentage rent. We believe that this type of rent is an incentive for the landlord to continually improve the marketability of the property so the retail tenant can enjoy higher sales. If minimum rent is the rent to simply occupy the space, then percentage rent can be seen as a license to access a market – those consumers attractive to the tenant - akin to a royalty or franchise fee.

Common Area Recoveries

Common area recoveries also go by several names, such as operating recoveries, OpEx, Common Area Maintenance or CAM (a misnomer if it includes property taxes) and Triple Net (or NNN). Before we discuss what this type of rent is, it is important to understand what is the common area.

Almost every lease will generally define the common area as that portion, or portions, of the property that can be used and enjoyed by all the tenants, their employees and customers or visitors. These include landscaped areas, parking facilities, patios, hallways, building chases, elevators and escalators, loading docks, etc. Essentially, any place or thing that serves more than one tenant. The definition is further cited as an area that is also not leased or intended to be leased.

The roof and exterior glazing are also generally parts of the common area.

Now this is important to keep in mind. The landlord has no legal or moral obligation to manage, maintain or operate the common areas of a property they own. They could just leave it to the tenant's themselves to attend to the common areas – and in fact, this is effectively what happens in a strata (also known as a condominium, or condo) property. The tenants would have to band together in some form to deal with all the things that make up the common areas of the property.

While not obligated, there are a host of reasons why the landlord wants to take care the common area. Briefly, these include control, expertise and efficiency.

The landlord will arrange and pay for services that affect the common area, such as janitorial and security (please see the recoveries chapter for a larger list). In turn the landlord expects to be reimbursed for these expenses as well as be compensated for their time and attention to the common areas so the tenants don't have to manage all these aspects themselves.

The costs associated with the common areas are far more volatile than the landlord's mortgage costs so they tend to change on a yearly basis. Prudent landlords want to stabilize the expense to the tenant as much as possible however, so there are no wild swings on the common area recoveries from one year to the next. Since the common area recovery is usually a monthly prepayment based on the annual common area operating expenses, a good landlord can manage the budget and smooth out the common area expenses by deferring or bringing forward certain work depending on whether the actual costs of operating the common areas are forecast to come in over or under the budget.

Here is a lease management principle that all lease administrators should practice, whether working for the landlord or the tenant:

> *Only those costs pertaining to the common areas and the common good of **all** the tenants of the property should be included in the common expense recovery billings.*

Property Tax Recovery

The landlord also wants to cover off the costs of property, or realty, tax. This is also an expense that changes annually over the term of the lease, just like common area recoveries, so it is a separate recovery. There are four very good reasons that the property tax recovery should **NOT** be included in the common area recovery and it should be established as a separate recovery item.

Reason #1

Property tax is the single largest expense at the property for many landlords. Permitting a tenant to pay a one-twelfth portion of the estimated tax bill in this case may cause a cash flow issue for the landlord. Therefore, the landlord may opt for a single annual billing to the tenant for its share of the overall taxes, when the landlord receives the tax bill. This single billing reduces the cash flow concern for the landlord but creates issues for the tenant. Here are two potential issues that lease administrators for tenants should take into consideration.

Unless the tenant has the reserves or has made a provision for the single tax bill from the landlord, the tenant may itself face a cash flow issue. If the lease contains an option for the landlord to issue one tax bill rather than having the tenant pay monthly, the tenant's lease administrator should bring this to the attention of senior management so the finance department can create appropriate provisions.

The second issue the tenant could face with a landlord's once annual billing of property taxes is a loss of its recovery of a portion of the taxes during a transfer of the lease or at the lease expiration.

Many governments that charge a property tax do so at the commencement of the government's fiscal year. As a result, the tenant is paying up front for the taxes for the year. If the tenant then transfers the lease or the lease expires, the tenant should receive a pro-rata share of the balance of that year's taxes. Therefore, the lease administrator should note the provision so the company is alerted to ask for the return of the appropriate amount of tax from the landlord or assignee, subtenant or transferee. Many landlords place the onus to ask for this refund on the tenant and a transferee may not be aware of the situation.

Reason #2
Property tax is typically not attributed to the common areas but to the tenant premises, or space.

You may find that there is a notation that common area expenses include property tax on the common area. That is a lease provision in case the government starts charging property tax on the common areas, but in most western jurisdictions there is no property tax attributed to that area. Why?

In many western countries the method of determining how much an income producing property pays in tax is determined using the income approach to assessment.

Since income-producing properties are valued and purchased based on the net operating income of the property, that is the same method a tax assessor uses, which, in turn and using a series of calculations, determines the tax bill.

The income for the property is derived from the space occupied by tenants and not the common area. In theory, the common landscaped areas, free parking areas and hallways don't have income and as such the tax assessor ignores those areas when making their calculations.

If you've followed me this far you will know that common area recoveries should only include a recovery for an expense the landlord makes relating to the common areas. Since there is no property tax on the common area, it is incorrect to include property tax as a common area recovery.

Reason #3
This is related to the way income-producing properties are assessed and billed property taxes too. We call this the Equitable Share concept and it should be included in all leases.

Most leases have the recovery of common area expenses and property taxes based on the area occupied by the tenant relative to the total leasable area of the property. For example, if the tenant occupies 1,000 square feet of space (ignoring gross ups and the definition of usable vs rentable space, as discussed in another chapter) in a building that had a total area of 100,000 square feet, this tenant would effectively pay 1% of the total expenses of the common areas and property taxes.

And that is the way the property tax bill is allocated by the landlord in most cases. But remember that the government assesses based on the income approach?

The assessor does this by obtaining the rent roll for the property and although the assessor is working on a 'whole property' basis it is the sum of the individual tenant rents that make up that total. The use of a proportionate share based on the area of the tenant space in relation to the total area means some tenants are paying more, or less, than they should in property tax, since not all tenants pay the same rent or occupy the same size of space. The following chart illustrates the issue.

Tenant	Area	Annual Rent	Area as a percentage of total area	Rent as a percentage of total rent
1	8,000	128,000	41%	25%
2	1,500	67,500	8%	13%
3	3,500	129,500	18%	26%
4	6,000	150,000	31%	30%
5	500	30,000	3%	6%
Total	19,500	505,000	100%	100%

If the property tax bill were allocated on a per square foot basis Tenant 1 would be responsible for 41% of the total bill. However, their rent only contributed 25% of the total income used to create that tax bill.

Only Tenant #4 would be about the same using either method, while the balance of the tenants would pay less on an area allocation basis.

The equitable share method of allocating property taxes does have its drawbacks. As a general rule of thumb the larger tenants and those who can negotiate a lower rent benefit at the expense of smaller tenants who may also suffer less income making the equitable share tax burden unmanageable for them.

The equitable share basis also means there is more volatility as rents change from one year to the next. This also increases the cost of management by the landlord, as there has to be an annual recalculation.

On the other hand, the equitable share method reflects how taxes are truly calculated and would be no different than the tax burden in a single tenant building.

Reason #4
How property taxes are calculated and collected is legislated and out of the hands of the landlord. While it is currently common for the government to issue just one property

tax bill per legal title property and let the landlord allocate the property taxes amongst their tenants, there is nothing to prevent the government to change its billing method, charging each tenant separately for their property taxes.

Therefore, there is additional wording in the lease that acknowledges that possibility.

Tenant Specific Recoveries
This can be a billing from the landlord to a tenant for a service provided to specifically that tenant, such as extra hours of lighting or HVAC, or tenant specific window cleaning or waste removal from the premises. It could also be a recovery of expenses related to a specific group of tenants but not all tenants.

Remember our principle related to common expense recoveries?

> *Only those costs pertaining to the common areas and the common good of all the tenants of the property should be included in the common expense recovery billings.*

The use of tenant specific recoveries facilitates that principle. However, it is even more useful.

Using tenant specific recoveries in the lease, the lease administrator can set up different pools of expenses and parameters for those expenses.

For example, lets assume waste removal from the tenants' spaces is currently (and we say incorrectly) included in common area expense recovery at an annual expense of $100,000 and the total leasable building area is 100,000 square feet. Therefore the cost and recovery of premises waste removal is $1.00 per square foot.

However, a waste audit found that 75% of the waste was coming from a restaurant in the building that only occupied 40% of the space and the remainder of the tenants produced only 25% of the waste.

Recovering premises waste removal on a per square foot basis through the common area expense recovery places an unfair burden of the waste removal cost on the non-restaurant tenants. Setting up a tenant specific recovery based on the waste audit solves that problem.

Now let's assume that in addition to the waste expense being recovered via common expense recovery on a per square foot basis, the property had a 10% vacancy factor. Since common area recoveries are generally calculated on the total leasable building area, the landlord would only be able to recover $90,000 of the total $100,000 cost of waste removal. This is a recovery slippage of $10,000 that will impact the landlord's net operating income. Setting up a tenant specific recovery based on the waste generated by the occupied space solves that problem because vacant space doesn't create waste. The landlord obtains full recovery.

Now let's assume that in addition to the waste expense being recovered via common expense recovery on a per square foot basis, the restaurant negotiated a cap on the common area expense recovery such that the landlord can only recovery 85 cents on each dollar of common area expenses. Setting up a tenant specific recovery based on the waste removal from that space also solves that problem, since the expense is completely removed from the capped common area expense recovery and is not impacted by it.

Using tenant specific recoveries is a very useful tool that should be in every lease and understood by every lease administrator.

Completely understanding the landlord's streams of income from a tenant's lease allows the lease administrator and the accounting staff to better manage the lease and the various expenses.

116

From the landlord's perspective it can mean a healthier bottom line with fewer tenant complaints about expense allocations.

From the tenant's lease administrator's point of view, the clearer each expense pool, the clearer it is to note and contest billing errors, which can be as high as 50% of landlord billings.

Chapter 10
CALCULATING PERCENTAGE
RENT AND BREAKPOINTS
(Natural and Artificial)

In Retail leases, Commercial real estate professionals should be aware of a common provision in leases known as Percentage Rent. The below chapter will explain how percentage rent and breakpoints calculated with clear examples along the way.

Percentage Rent:
This chapter explains how the percentage rent and breakpoints. In Retail Leases, Tenant needs to pay to Landlord Percentage Rent in addition to Base Rent.

Rent paid by a retail tenant which is based upon a percentage of Gross Sales in excess of a specified dollar amount (the Breakpoint). Also called 'Overage Rent'.

Types of Breakpoints:
Percentage rent provisions use either a natural or artificial breakpoint.

119

Natural Breakpoint:
The amount of Breakpoint which, when multiplied by the Overage Percentage, equals Annual Base Rent. Stated differently, a natural breakpoint is calculated as Annual Base Rent divided by the Overage or Percentage Rent Percentage. It is the point where the amount of percentage rent is equal to the amount of annual base rent.

A "natural breakpoint" is simply defined as the fixed annual rent amount divided by the percentage given.

A "natural" breakpoint occurs when the tenant pays his base rent OR "x" percent of sales, whichever is more.

Formula: Breakpoint = Yearly Base Rent / Sales Percentage

Artificial Breakpoint:
If a breakpoint is not natural it is called and "Artificial Breakpoint" In this case the amount of the breakpoint is stated as a fixed Gross Sales amount or Gross Sales per square foot and is fixed based upon negotiation between the landlord and tenant. Below are examples that illustrate the Percentage Rent calculation for Natural and Artificial Breakpoint.

1. Natural Breakpoint:

In addition to Minimum Rent, Tenant agrees to pay Percentage Rent to Landlord on a monthly basis, commencing the month in which Tenant's cumulative Gross Sales for the applicable Lease Year shall first exceed the Breakpoint during the Lease Year. Percentage Rent shall mean a sum equal to the Percentage Rent Rate of all Gross Sales in excess of the Breakpoint during each Lease Year. Percentage Rent Rate in this example is 6%. Breakpoint shall be an amount equal to the quotient of the Minimum Rent payable during the applicable Lease Year divided by the Percentage Rent Rate. Minimum Rent shall be $180,000/annum.

For the above example, Natural Breakpoint is $3,000,000, which was determined by dividing the Minimum Rent by the Percentage rent rate ($180,000/6%).

Calculating the Natural Breakpoint is the first step to determine if the tenant pays any Percentage Rent. If the Gross Sales for the particular year is $4,000,000, then Percentage Rent the tenant pays would be $60,000. We get this by subtracting the Breakpoint from the sales and multiplying the difference by the Percentage Rent rate. The formula looks like this:

(($4,000,000-$3,000,000)*6%)

2. Artificial Breakpoint:

Tenant signs a five-year lease that requires tenant to pay Base Rent of $50,000/annum plus Percentage Rent in an amount of 4% of Gross Sales provided those Gross Sales are in excess of $1,500,000.

For the above example, the Breakpoint was negotiated when the lease was created and set at an arbitrary amount of $1,500,000. If the Gross Sales for the particular year is $3,000,000, then Percentage Rent shall be $60,000. Once again, we get this by subtracting the Breakpoint from the sales and multiplying the difference by the Percentage Rent rate. The formula looks like this:

(($3,000,000-$1,500,000)*4%).

Here are some other things the Lease administrator should look for concerning percentage rent.

There are many variables to the way percentage rent can be calculated. The most common is whether or not percentage rent is calculated annually, or on some shorter period such as quarterly or monthly. And if it is calculated on a shorter period of time than a full year, is it calculated on a **cumulative** or **direct** basis. Here is the difference as illustrated in the examples below:

Lets assume in both cases that the minimum rent is $24,000 per annum, or $2,000 per month. Lets also assume that the percentage rent rate is 8% of gross sales.

The point at which $24,000 is equal to 8% of sales is $300,000; or $25,000 per month. This is called the natural breakpoint.

Lets further assume that the tenant has sales of $26,000 in the first month, $20,500 in the second month and $27,500 in the third month.

If the percent rent is calculated monthly on a **cumulative** basis over a year, the math looks like this chart.

Month	Sales	Cumulative Sales	8% of sales to date	Minimum Rent to date	Percentage rent payable
1	$26,000	$26,000	$2080	$2,000	$80
2	20,500	46,500	3,720	4,000	-
3	27,500	74,000	5,920	6,000	-

Using the cumulative basis you aggregate both the sales to date, apply the percentage rent rate calculation and subtract the sum of the minimum rent to date. Alternatively, subtract the cumulative monthly break point from the sum of the sales to date and if the answer is negative, no percentage rent is payable. As you can see the sales in the first month resulted in percentage rent being payable. In the third month there is no percentage rent payable even though the sales were higher than in the first month. In reality, even the $80.00 would be refunded by the landlord if this trend continued as the total annual sales would be below the breakpoint for the year.

If the percentage rent was calculated only on the month's sales (the **direct** method), the math looks like the following chart.

Month	Sales	8% of sales for the month	Minimum Rent for the month	Percentage rent payable
1	$26,000	$2,080	$2,000	$80
2	20,500	1,640	2,000	-
3	27,500	2,200	2,000	$200

The total owed by the tenant is $280.00 for the period and the landlord wouldn't have to refund any of the payments because the percentage rent payable exceeds the minimum rent, or alternatively the sales each month exceed the monthly breakpoint.

Of course, which method that is used is determined by the way the lease is worded. The lease may not describe the method as the "Cumulative Method" or "Direct Method" but will describe the math and may use the word 'cumulative' in the formula if it is to be calculated on that basis.

The percentage rent factor can also be split at different sales levels; or different factors can be assigned to different categories of merchandise carried by the tenant, based on the gross margin of each category.

The table below outlines typical percentage rent factors used in the retail industry.

TYPICAL PERCENTAGE RENTS

Card & gift shop	5.0 to 8.0%
Drugstore	2.5 to 4.0%
Liquor and wine shop	1.5 to 5.0%
Pet shop	5.0 to 8.0%
Restaurant	4.0 to 7.0%
Supermarket	1.0 to 2.0%

Adapted from *Dollars & Cents of Shopping Centers*, Urban Land Institute, Washington, D.C.

These types of complicated percentage rent calculations are not typical, and so we won't go into length in this book about them. However, take heart if you run across one as they all use the same principals outlined in this chapter.

Chapter 11
WHAT ARE RECOVERIES?

Have you seen these words and acronyms?

Commercial Operating Expenses (OE), Common Area Maintenance Expenses (CAM) and Real Estate Tax (RET) Recoveries

So what are recoveries?

When a Landlord leases space to a Tenant, the operating expenses to repair and maintain the property are included in the calculation of the cost per square foot. Recovery of these expenses, also known as pass-through expenses, is an important aspect of the economic value of each Lease and the property as a whole and most likely a major factor in lease negotiations. The method for recovering expenses are typically identified by the type of property in question, though there are instances where lease negotiations may result in an atypical recovery clause in a Lease.

Expenses incurred by a Landlord to lease space, including commissions, legal fees, architectural fees and similar Landlord expenses are not pass-through expenses. Expenses specifically incurred on behalf of a single tenant or a group of tenants that does not include all tenants is recovered from only from those who benefit.

Does a Landlord make a profit from recoveries?

The intent of recovering operating expenses is typically and should always be spelled out in a Lease as just that – a recovery of actual expenses incurred by the Landlord to run a property in the manner in which the Tenants are entitled to expect. The exception might be in a retail setting where, pursuant to a Lease, an administrative fee is added to the expenses. This fee is to cover some or all of the overhead involved in both procuring the services and products on which monies were spent (property management), as well as the cost of the accounting (property accounting). This method is typically used along with the triple net method of recoveries, as opposed to expenses recovered over a base year (methods of recovery calculations are discussed in detail further along in the chapter.

What methods exist for recovering operating expenses?

Base Year (sometimes called Full Service)

For most commercial (office) Leases, the method typically referred to as Full Service recovers expenses over the Base Year's expenses. The initial Base Rent includes the operating expenses for the Base Year (typically year of Lease Execution), and future years' operating expenses over that Base Year's expenses will be passed through to the Tenant based on Tenant's pro rata share of the building. Often the expenses considered to be controllable by the Landlord– typically all expenses **except** Utilities, Snow Removal, Insurance and Taxes, or those expenses for which, outside of efforts to obtain the lowest rates possible when possible, are required to be incurred – are limited by a cap on the percent increase allowable year to year. For example, the cap language may state that controllable expenses cannot be increased in excess of 5% over the prior year's expenses. If the total controllable expenses for the Base Year were $200,000, then the controllable expenses for the following, comparison, year cannot exceed $210,000.

Another concept typically included in commercial leases is that of gross up. Expenses that vary based on average occupancy during the year are often grossed up to reflect Tenant's share had the property been 95% or 100% occupied. Since Tenant's share is calculated by dividing the entire building square footage by the premises square footage, the recovery of such expenses variable based on occupancy must be grossed up in order to recover Tenant's true share of the expense incurred. The expenses typically grossed up are Utilities, with the exception of common area (i.e., parking lot lights, since that usage does not vary by occupancy); Janitorial expenses for the building, typically passed through at 95% or 100% of the actual contract cost per square foot, with the exception of common area porter services, (which are unlikely to vary based on occupancy), and interior and exterior window cleaning (also not variable based on occupancy as the entire building is cleaned regardless of occupancy).

Triple Net (NNN)

In the case of retail and industrial leases, operating expenses are typically recovered on a Triple Net (NNN) basis, wherein the Tenant is responsible for its share of all common area expenses based on its prorate share of the project. The Base Rent for NNN Leases does not include operating expenses; it is reduced from the full service rate by the current year's budgeted expenses per square foot. Hence, Tenants are responsible for their share, sometimes calculated on Gross Leasable Area (GLA), sometimes 95% or 100% of Grossed Leasable Occupied Area (GLOA), which is comparable to the 95% or 100% gross up method used in commercial (office) leases. In a retail setting, there are often anchor stores which are 10,000 sf or more. To equitably share the expenses for the shopping center, the square footage of any anchor store, as defined in an individual Tenant's lease, will be deducted from the total center square footage when calculating the non-anchor Tenants' pro rata share. For example, if the property is 200,000 square feet, and there are two anchor stores, one of 10,000 sf, the other 25,000 sf, the denominator used to calculate the non-anchor tenants' shares will be 200,000-10,000-25,000, or 165,000sf.

Which expenses are typically recovered, and how?

Following is a list of Operating Expenses *(Uncontrollable expenses are in italics)* which by no means is all-inclusive:

Categories:

Administrative
Miscellaneous Administrative
Administrative Salaries
Administrative Taxes and Benefits
Telephone
Management Fees

Utilities
Electricity
Water & Sewer
Gas
Oil

Contracts
Snow and Ice Removal
Landscaping & Grounds Contract
Landscaping & Grounds Supplies
Janitorial Contract
Janitorial Supplies
Parking Lot Sweeping/Policing
Porter Service
Security
Trash Removal
Window Cleaning

Repairs and Maintenance (R&M)
Asphalt and Concrete

Doors and Windows
Engineering Wages
Engineering Benefits
R&M Electrical
R&M HVAC
R&M General
R&M Generator
R&M Parking Lot
R&M Plumbing
R&M Lights and Fixtures

Insurance

Real Estate Taxes

Taxes and Licenses - Other

Of these expenses those which may be subject to gross up are the expenses which will vary as occupancy/vacancy in the property varies. Expenses may be both uncontrollable and subject to gross up. For example, utilities including electricity, gas, oil, water & sewer, are both uncontrollable and subject to gross up. Janitorial contract expense is a gross up expense, and, with greater frequency, management fees are grossed up. Again, the basis for determining whether an expense is grossed up is whether it rises and falls as occupancy increases and decreases.

Tenants are often concerned about being billed by a Landlord for expenses recovered from other Tenants. In any case where one or more Tenant is billed based on sub-metered usage, that income will reduce the expense. For example, in the case of a Tenant with a large computer room which is separately sub-metered for electricity, the amount billed back to that particular Tenant will be reduced from the total electricity expense passed through to all Tenants.

Caps on Controllable Expenses

Many leases are negotiated to include a percent cap on controllable expenses over either a base year's expense or over the prior year, depending on the language. Cap language has a tendency to be ambiguous and should be carefully read and re-read before finalizing any lease with a cap. Caps may be a fixed percentage from year to year, where controllable expenses in the first comparison year cannot exceed the base year by 5%, and in the next comparison year cannot exceed the first comparison year's expenses by 5% and so forth throughout the lease term. This method is the easiest to calculate, and also is the least likely to be seen in a lease.

In another, less common method, the cap percentage itself increases each year over the initial, base percentage of, for example 2.5%, by 5% each year. This results in a fixed, schedule of annual caps. This method may be referred to as a cumulative cap however this is a misnomer.

In the case of a cumulative cap, the percentage by which controllable operating expenses are capped over the previous calendar year is defined, i.e., 5%. Uncontrollable expenses are excluded from the capped expenses, and typically include utility costs, snow removal costs, insurance costs, real property tax increases and any other costs beyond If such expenses have increased by more than 5% in a previous calendar year and by less than 5% in a subsequent calendar year, LL has the right to pass through the increase LL was unable to pass through in the previous calendar year in the subsequent calendar year provided that LL does not exceed in any year a maximum increase of 5%.

Pro rata shares

Tenants pro rata shares are typically calculated by dividing the number of leased square feet by the number of square feet in the property or project. For example, a tenant with 10,000sf of a 200,000sf office building is responsible for 5% of the operating expenses incurred for the building.

Often the share is subject to change based on changes in measurement that can occur, for example, when a full-floor suite is split into multiple suites with common area hallways and restrooms. At this point, the individual premises are re-measured and the total square feet of the floor will change.

In cases were an expense is incurred for the benefit of one tenant or a specific group of tenants, that expense will be shared only by those who benefit. It is possible for a single Tenant to pay different percentages (shares) of some expenses than it does for others. If an electric meter services one building of a multi-building strip shopping center, the share for each of the Tenants in that particular strip will be calculated based on the Premises square footage divided by the square footage of only that portion of the center. That same Tenant's share of parking lot maintenance expense, on the other hand, may be calculated by dividing the Tenant's premises square feet by the entire property's square feet, resulting in a smaller share of a larger expense.

Summary

Operating expenses and real estate taxes are an important aspect of the economic value of each Lease and the property as a whole and most likely a major factor in lease negotiations. It is important that the various methods for recovering expenses are considered and understood by all parties involved in negotiating and preparing a lease.

Since recoveries are so heavily negotiated and both parties want to make sure they are correct, it is important that the Lease Administrator sets up the recoveries for each tenant correctly. Mistakes can be costly both in financial terms as well as credibility and tenant relations.

Chapter 12
CALCULATING THE DAYS
OF THE MONTH

Calculating the days of the month may sound like it isn't worthy of this book, but there are frequent errors.

For example, the tenant has a 45 day rent-free fixturing period that started on March 1. What is the first day rent would start? The answer is April 15. Straight forward.

But if that same 45 day rent free period started on April 1, the first day rent would start would not be May 15th. It would be May 16th.

For good measure, we will throw in the varying days in the month of February, depending on the Leap Year, and one can quickly see the importance of correctly counting the days of the month.

People often think in terms of 30 - 60 - 90 day increments when thinking of one, two or three months, but using these common 'standards' for things such as rent free periods creates odd days and additional lease management and accounting time calculating per diem rates, etc. Instead, use the appropriate number of days, such as 30, 31, 61, 91 and 92. Don't forget that the period will be shorter if the month of February is included; and the two months of July and August together contain a combined 62 days.

Many times a lease will state that if a lease starts on a day other than the first of the month, the lease will end on the last day of the corresponding month at the end of the term, or the end of the first anniversary of the commencement date will be the last day of that month. For example, if the lease started July 7th the last day of the first anniversary or the term, as the case may be, would be July 31st.

Using these two different wording options and assuming a five year term that started July 7; the actual length for the first year would be 1 year and 25 days and the total term would be 5 years and 25 days, depending on the actual lease wording. Don't forget that a period that starts on one date, such as the 7th day in this example, expires on the preceding date at the end of the period, such as the 6th in this example.

It is always good practice to word the lease so that the first year of the term ends at the end of the month irrespective of when it started; otherwise, the lease administrator and accounting staff will have to manage partial month calculations throughout the entire term. This isn't an issue if the rent remains unchanged over the term; but it will add management time and may cause potential errors if there are any changes in the lease rates tied to the anniversary of the start of any year of the lease. For example, lets assume the lease didn't have the wording we just suggested, and the rent increases on each anniversary of the lease commencement date. We will also assume the lease commenced on the 10th of the month. The result would be the lease administrator and the accounting staff would have to calculate one rent on a per diem basis for the first nine days prior to the anniversary date each year and another per diem rent for the balance of the month. Each calendar year the tenant would have up to three different monthly rental amounts: The old monthly rent before the anniversary month, the (split) rent for the anniversary month itself, and the new rent after the anniversary month.

Per Diem

Per diem is a Latin phrase meaning "by the day". It is important to check the definition of per diem in the specific lease you are working on at the time. While most leases define the calculation of per diem as 1 divided by the days in a year (365), some use the calculation of 1 divided by the days of the applicable month (28, 29, 30 or 31, as the case may be. There is no universal doctrine for how a per diem is calculated so always check the specific lease.

Calculating the correct number of days in the month is also important if the tenant has a window to perform an act; such as, exercising the option to renew no less than 180 days prior to the lease expiration.

It is also important to understand and know the significance between calendar days, business days and clear days. Generally speaking and unless defined in the lease otherwise, these are the accepted definitions:

Calendar days are the number of days in the run of the calendar and include Saturdays, Sundays and public holidays.

Business days typically refer to the workweek of weekdays, Monday to Friday and *exclude* Saturdays, Sundays and public holidays. It is important to note that on a regional and global scale the workweek and the business days vary. For example, there is a public holiday in Canada on July 1 called Canada Day that is not recognized in the USA. Conversely, Independence Day on July 4 is a public holiday in the USA that is not recognized in Canada, and England does not recognize either July 1 or July 4 as a public holiday. Therefore it is always good practice, if using "Business day," to further define it, including the region it pertains to so there is no confusion when dealing with an international portfolio.

Clear days refer to full and complete days. This entails, in a computation of days, the exclusion of the first and last days, as is the accepted definition in Canada, England and the USA. For example, there are six clear days between Sunday and the following Sunday.

Knowing which is which is important for items such as notices, application of interest charges, etc.

The chart on the next page is a handy reference to the number of calendar days remaining in a month at the end of a day. February is not included in the charts. Please consider Leap Years when calculating.

For Months with **30** Days	
At the end of	*Remaining days*
1	29
2	28
3	27
4	26
5	25
6	24
7	23
8	22
9	21
10	20
11	19
12	18
13	17
14	16
15	15
16	14
17	13
18	12
19	11
20	10
21	9
22	8
23	7
24	6
25	5
26	4
27	3
28	2
29	1
30	

For Months with **31** Days	
At the end of	*Remaining days*
1	30
2	29
3	28
4	27
5	26
6	25
7	24
8	23
9	22
10	21
11	20
12	19
13	18
14	17
15	16
16	15
17	14
18	13
19	12
20	11
21	10
22	9
23	8
24	7
25	6
26	5
27	4
28	3
29	2
30	1
31	

Chapter 13
RENEWAL OPTIONS

An option to renew the Lease falls under the broad category of Tenant Benefit Clauses because it is a clause requested by the Tenant that only benefits the Tenant. It is an option that, unless otherwise stated, is exclusively under the Tenant's control.

Here is a major concern about an option to renew the lease that seems to be lost on many landlords as it appears in almost every lease where the option has been granted. An option to renew the lease is just that. It is an opportunity for the tenant to renew the legal contract it negotiated for a further term.

Most times, options are provided in the initial lease negotiated between the landlord and the tenant. Consider the relative negotiating strength of that first lease. The landlord is typically 'selling' the tenant on the property and the knowledgeable tenant is unsure of their performance and will want to mitigate its risk. As a result, there are perhaps more concessions given by the landlord, than when the property has proven itself to the tenant.

If it is a good location, the tenant will want to lock in those concessions. If it is a mediocre to poor location, the tenant will simply not exercise its option in order to further negotiate the lease with the landlord or relocate.

Another issue with renewing the lease document, is that things change over the term of the lease, despite the lease negotiators' best attempts to make the lease as flexible as possible. Laws can change that affect the operations of the property, zoning can change, tenant-merchandising practices evolve and technologies are invented. Notice too that all these examples are beyond the direct control of the landlord.

There are still leases in effect today that date back before the days of personal computers, let alone the internet and there are leases that predate grocery stores providing prepared meals, drugs or clothing.

From the landlord's perspective it now has leases that may cause leasing, operating and financial concerns due to these types of changes.

Landlords also want to position their asset favorably in the event of a sale. Many landlords like to use their own lease form after purchasing a property. By limiting the current lease to the initial term vs. the term and all the options means a purchaser can 'convert' the tenant to their lease form sooner. While probably a minor consideration, it is still one to note.

Many tenants simply ask for the renewal option because they want to secure their tenancy in the property. They don't want to be in a lease that is 5 to 10 years long, build the business and find they no longer have their location to enjoy their hard work or to reap the rewards and sell the business. The Tenant should always ask for a number of options.

To limit renewal options, the landlord should establish a guide concerning which types of tenants are granted the option and which are not. As a rule of thumb, single store specialty stores should not be granted options; or, if required, at most a single option provided.

Restaurants typically require a series of options due to the capital intensive nature of their business; national chains and anchor tenants will always demand a number of options.

Renewal of Lease, or.......

Since options only work in the tenant's favor, the question needs to be asked about an alternative that is more in the landlord's favor if you work for the landlord. Or at least is more on balance in protecting the landlord risks.

The answer comes in two parts. It depends on what is being renewed and how it is structured.

In many cases, the tenant is simply asking for security of the space. Therefore, the landlord should offer a renewal of the <u>tenancy</u>, not a renewal of the lease. The renewal of tenancy lets the tenant know they can secure the space, but the underlying lease document is not being renewed and a new document must be negotiated near the end of the term.

This allows the landlord to accomplish two things: the landlord can update the lease if needed, and the landlord can assess their relative negotiating strength and claw-back earlier concessions.

The renewal of tenancy clause the Greenstead Consulting Group advise our clients to use states that the tenant will sign the landlord's then standard lease. We use this wording specifically. On the face of it, all lease wording negotiation is removed at the renewal and the tenant must sign the standard lease as presented. In practice, we use this to retain negotiating leverage and, depending on the negotiations, provide some concessions and/or trade concessions for higher rent.

If there must be a renewal in the document, a renewal of tenancy is always more in the Landlord's favor than a renewal of the actual lease. Tenants should also be aware of the leverage a renewal of tenancy provides the landlord and should resist that wording.

The landlord will tend to structure the renewal in such a way that the landlord doesn't end up in a worse position than it was in prior to the renewal.

Typically, landlords place conditions on the tenant's ability to exercise the renewal other than to simply provide notice.

Some key conditions include:
- The tenant must be the tenant originally named in the lease, or (if need be) an approved assignee. The

option to renew was granted to the original tenant at the time of the initial negotiation. It may have come up because that specific tenant was a desirable tenant and had the negotiating power.

- The tenant must be in full and continuous occupation of the premises and be conducting business on a daily basis. This is one of those items that can easily catch the landlord off guard if they don't cross check their concessions and clauses.

If the tenant has the ability to cease operating from the premises but continue to control the premises under the lease, the landlord certainly doesn't want to allow that tenant to be able to exercise a renewal. This is particularly true if the tenant also enjoys a restrictive covenant in the lease.

- The tenant must not have been in default or breach of the lease. This is usually worded as broadly as possible even though many tenants will push back and ask that the wording be modified so that the tenant can't be in default at the time of renewal.

- The renewal clause may have some form of performance criteria before the tenant is allowed to renew the lease. The reasoning is landlord should only grant renewal options to tenants that benefit the business objectives of the landlord and the well being of the property. In a retail property the performance clause could be a formula tied to the tenant's sales and the sales of the property, a minimum gross revenue threshold, or the payment of percent rent.

- Likewise, the renewal may also be tied to a refurbishment of the premises depending on the initial term and the extent of the original leasehold improvements.

Setting Minimum Rent on Renewal

The second thing that must be done during the initial lease is outline how the minimum rent for the renewal period will be determined. Establishing the amount of minimum rent payable during the renewal term is sometimes more difficult than agreeing to the minimum rent for the initial term. On one hand the tenant wants rent that is either below or at the market rent they would have to pay at the time of the renewal. On the other hand, the landlord wants minimum rent that is at least the same rent they would obtain from another party at the time of the renewal, and preferably higher.

The obvious issue is that neither party has an accurate crystal ball as to what rents will be in 5 or more years in the future.

To mitigate the rent risk tenants ask for either a pre-negotiated rent amount they feel comfortable with; or 'fair market rent'. In the latter case, the tenant will want to have a third party, such as an arbitrator or mediator, determine what 'fair market rent' is to be if the two sides can't agree. Some tenants will negotiate hard for the lesser of the pre-negotiated rent or the fair market rent.

None of these options are good for the landlord as they are typically written. Remember that the renewal option itself is only beneficial to the tenant, so these types of rent structures only compound the issue for the landlord.

The detriments of pre-negotiated rents and 'lesser of' formulas are self explanatory. But how can a fair market rent be detrimental to the landlord? Most people would argue that the landlord should achieve what the general market bears and therefore the landlord will be in no worse position. Indeed most leases are written with 'fair market rent' clauses that capture the general rent in the marketplace.

However, if the landlord has a unique property, and has taken steps to lay claim to a unique market that only that property can access, then general market rent should not apply.

Why is this important?

The landlord can only control their own property. A nearly identical property - and space - in terms of size, configuration, community, etc. may have widely different rent than the landlord has for their property. The rent at the other property may be negatively influenced by any number of things including: high recoverable expenses, owner's lack of market knowledge, a desire by the owner to provide some form of loss leader, etc.

Therefore, the landlord negotiating the renewal is attempting to manage and control *their* asset based on the actions (and agendas) of *other* landlords who do not have an interest in this property. Additionally, the tenant is comparing the rent of other properties that is not the property under negotiation.

This is not a sustainable business model for the Landlord, yet it is perpetuated in lease after lease.

Of course, the other property may also have higher rent but the tenant will immediately discount that property and seek other properties with rents that are less than our landlord is seeking in order to support the tenant's negotiating position.

Obviously, the tenant has the stronger negotiating position when using fair market rent.

To retain the landlord's position and to accurately reflect that the rent for the renewal period is for the property the tenant actually occupies, the landlord can agree that the rent would be the same rent the landlord would otherwise obtain for that space or a comparable space in that specific property. That is the fair rent for <u>that</u> space.

Other Considerations
It may sometimes become necessary to renew the lease document rather than the tenancy. In those cases, it is important for the landlord, their asset manager, property manager, lease administrator, etc. to review the original lease and insert wording in the lease extension document that removes

landlord obligations that only occurred for the initial lease such as leasing incentives, construction allowances, free rent, etc. as well as noting what new obligations the tenant may have, such as a refurbishment of the premises, if part of the renewal provisions.

Whether renewing or extending the lease document or the tenancy it is also important to note that the number of remaining options is reduced by one. If there was only one option, then it should be specifically noted in the document that there are no further renewal options.

Term

Of course, renewals are all about the Term, or length, of the lease. Leasing is seasonal in nature, as tenants want the space in order to open in time for their respective busiest season. For example, a tax preparer will want to open at the beginning of the tax season, not after, in order to capitalize on the initial good cash flow. Retailers tend to want to open for the fall since the vast majority of their positive cash flow occurs in the last weeks of the year. Of course, there are businesses that have fairly consistent year round cash flow, such as doctors and many lawyers.

There is no rule in leasing that states that the term must be in equal annual increments such as 5 years or 10 years. As a result a tenant may want to negotiate a term of X years and Y months so the term starts just before their positive cash flow season and end just before the negative cash flow season. There can be several reasons for this, but the strongest is the leverage it gives the tenant for the renewal negotiation.

Returning to the retail example, most retailers have negative cash flow commencing in January or February each year. The cash flow improves in Spring and dips down again in summer. A savvy retail tenant will recognize that if they do not renew a lease that ends at the start of a negative cash flow period and vacate the building it may mean the landlord will have that vacancy for some time before it is released, resulting in lost income for the landlord. This holds true even if the tenant is required to give six months notice of its intension to exercise a renewal option or not.

Both parties should be aware of the seasonality of the tenant's business and use that knowledge to their advantage.

Notices to Renew

Except for the rare 'evergreen lease' that renews automatically, every renewal option contains either a window in which a tenant may exercise the option to renew, such as a period of time between two dates, or a last date of the term to exercise the option.

In either case the wording will most likely state the exercise must be made a *number of days* prior to the expiration of the term rather than by a specific date. For example, if the tenant has a window in which to exercise the option to renew the wording may look like this:

If the Tenant gives the Landlord not more than twelve (12) months nor less than six (6) months' written notice prior to the expiry of the initial Term or of any extension thereof......

or

If the Tenant gives the Landlord not more than one hundred eighty (180) days nor less than ninety (90) days' written notice prior to the expiry of the initial Term or of any extension thereof........

If the tenant has to provide notice by a certain date, the wording may look like this:

If the Tenant gives the Landlord not less than six (6) months' written notice prior to the expiry of the initial Term or of any extension thereof....

Or it could be expressed in days and not months, as in the previous example.

All this is important because renewal options are often missed because the notification to renew was incorrect or wasn't sent at all. Landlords count on the tenant missing the deadline for exercising their option to renew. Therefore, it is very important to create a flag for the renewal option in whatever professional, centralized system you are using to manage your leases. It is not enough to put a reminder in a computer calendar software. The person managing that calendar may leave and others may forget to transfer the calendar information.

One last note about Notices. Don't forget that when the lease calls for a written notice, the professional lease administrator will check the Notices section of the lease to determine the following:

- The methods acceptable for a written notice,
- To verify the address for the landlord,
- The time period before a Notice is 'deemed' to be received. This period

needs to be included when calculating the window. For example, the tenant must give notice no later than 90 days prior to the end of the term and a mailed notice is deem received 5 days after postmark. The prudent lease administrator will ensure the last date for a mailed notice is 95 days prior to the end of the term, and preferably more.

Chapter 14
USE CLAUSES AND EXCLUSIVITIES

In reading thousands of leases it seems that the clause that outlines the permitted use of the premises does not get the attention it deserves. This is particularly true in a retail property.

An effective retail property relies on three attributes: merchandising, massing and market. The Landlord relies on these three attributes, and each tenant's use clause plays a significant role in designing the merchandising of the property.

Here is an actual, poorly written use clause from a lease:

"...the Premises will be solely for the purpose of a licensed sit-down restaurant and for take out and delivery and a lounge. The cuisine

will be primarily Middle Eastern, Western and European. "

There are many business issues with this clause including a lack of clarity around what constitutes any of the listed cuisine types.

A good use clause on the other hand should be detailed and yet broad enough to permit the tenant merchandising scope within their business concept.

An excellent way to do this is to create a hierarchy of the primary use, a secondary or ancillary use(s) and, in some situations, common products. In each case, it is always best to list the products, merchandise or services sold rather than the general concept. For example, the wording should be something along the lines of:

" the primary use is the sale at retail of [followed by a list of products or services that will make up the bulk of the business], and as ancillary to such primary use the sale at retail of [another list of complimentary product lines]."

Since retail concepts evolve and change it is always better to focus on the types of products and services rather than defaulting to a generic term for a concept. A prime

162

example –though there are many – is "women's wear". There are casual, athletic, petite, larger size, fast fashion, designer, maternity, bridal, uniform, mature, yoga and other types of specialty retailers under the broad definition of women's wear.

To properly merchandise the property and to avoid internal competition from tenants cannibalizing another tenant's sales, it is important to distinguish between the various types of "women's wear" in administering the lease.

A properly constructed use clause that has each tenant's product mix well defined also avoids the internal competition that occurs when the property has several similar categories of merchants. Not only does this aid in good tenant relations, because tenant "A" can't accuse the Landlord of duplicating their use and killing their business by leasing to tenant "B", but it should prompt market expansion since the two tenants aren't after the identical customer.

This is an important point when considering the merchandising mix of the property and is part of the second attribute of massing. Consider the potential success of a property that is focused on women's wear and the different merchants reflect each of the individual segments noted above from casual wear to yoga apparel as compared to a property where each of the tenants have overlapping products as they chase the same customers. If each tenant is targeted to a sub-section of the women's wear category then you will have massing.

If the property has multiple on-premise consumption food tenants in close proximity, such as a food court or restaurant area, it is even more important to segregate the product offering of each tenant to provide the customer with a breadth of choice and to avoid product infighting between operators.

One way to handle this is to add a third category to the use clause to handle all the items they all have in common such a beverages. Here is an example of how this works. We will assume that the property has a burger operation, a fish and chip operation, a sandwich shop and a Mexican restaurant.

If we were to chart the uses, it might look like the one on the following page, in very broad terms.

Tenant	Primary Use	Ancillary Use	Common Use
Burger	Hamburgers, Chicken Burgers	Fish Burgers, Veggie Burgers and French Fries	Pop, Water, Coffee, Tea, etc.
Fish & Chips	Deep Fried Fish, Grilled Fish, Fries served with these items	French Fries (sold individually), Fish Burgers and Fish Sandwiches	Pop, Water, Coffee, Tea, etc.
Sandwich	A variety of sandwiches (all named)	Fish Sandwiches, Salads (named), Soup	Pop, Water, Coffee, Tea, etc.
Mexican	A variety of Mexican entrees (all named)	Taco Salad, Tortilla Soup	Pop, Water, Coffee, Tea, etc.

Notice how the primary use – the product that accounts for the majority of sales – for the burger operation excludes fish burgers but the fish burger is listed as an ancillary item. Likewise the fish and chip shop also has the fish burger as an ancillary item.

All the tenants recognize that the items listed in the common use will be universally sold.

While all this may seem like additional work with little real benefit, it eases the management time in managing the merchandise mix, provides clarity around the leasing function and merchandise mix, and is most helpful if the landlord must provide an exclusivity covenant.

A strong, well worded use clause benefits both the landlord and the tenant.

RESTRICTIVE USE or EXCLUSIVE USE COVENANT

A restrictive use or exclusive use covenant is another example of a Tenant Benefit Clause™ (also known as a "TBC") that only benefits the tenant. Effectively, the covenant works to limit competition in the property.

Regional and national tenants will push hard for as many tenant benefit clauses as possible, particularly those that affect their sales performance. Remember that after the basic financial terms have been agreed to the balance of the lease is risk mitigation. Having the sole right to sell something in the property is a sales risk mitigation tool used by the tenant.

If the landlord is placed in the position where they must entertain an exclusivity, then the following is important, but often overlooked.

The restrictive covenant should be limited to the following two items only:

1. It should be limited only to the act of the landlord leasing another space in the property to a competing use. Leasing is the landlord's business, nothing more in this case. Many use clauses erroneously refer to the landlord not permitting any other tenant to use, occupy, stock, or sell or carry on business as "X,Y,Z." The "X,Y,Z" is typically worded as a general concept, which we have already agreed is a bad idea in a use clause from the landlord's perspective. It is worse in an exclusive covenant.

2. It should be limited only to the primary use of the tenant. This drives the restriction to products and not concepts. It also protects the landlord's ability to introduce other merchants that don't directly compete, but may have some overlapping merchandise or services as ancillary uses, as illustrated above.

Any agreement on a restrictive should exclude all anchor tenants, since they generally have very broad use clauses due to their size and nature of business.

Any existing tenants in the property should be excluded too, since it would be a monumental and expensive task to have an existing tenant unwind their merchandising. Likewise, from the landlord's point of view all of the existing tenants' heirs, assigns, successors and replacements should also be excluded so the current merchandising can be retained. From the tenant's point of view the exclusion shouldn't automatically apply to assigns and certainly not to replacements. Your lawyer will have appropriate wording.

Recall the poorly worded use clause example? This tenant also had a poorly worded restrictive covenant according to the landlord. The tenant on the other hand felt it was a good restrictive covenant. Here is what it said:

"....the Landlord shall not lease any other premises in the Shopping Centre to any other restaurant whose cuisine is similar to the cuisine offered by the tenant."

Between the use clause and the restrictive covenant, this tenant enjoyed a near monopoly on eat-in, take out or delivery service. The possible exception may be various styles of Asian food. Due to an overlapping grocery anchor restriction, the landlord was also restricted in leasing to food related businesses not deemed as restaurants. Consequently, the landlord was severely handcuffed in their leasing efforts and had to turn away many able and willing tenants resulting in a sustained loss of revenue and ultimately a loss in value when they sold the property. The purchaser simply used the tenant's restrictive covenant as a negotiation point on the price.

Other items to consider when dealing with a restrictive covenant and asking your lawyer to draft a restrictive covenant clause if you work for a landlord:

- The clause should be personal to the tenant.
- The clause should only apply while the tenant is in full and continuous occupation of the space. No landlord wants a tenant who has 'gone dark' to continue to affect the merchandising in the balance of the property.
- The clause should only apply if the tenant is not in breach or default of the lease.
- The clause should be removed or at least suspended if the tenant is on any form of rent relief. Rent relief is the antithesis for the reason for an exclusivity clause. A prudent asset manager should consult with the lease administrator to determine if there are any TBCs that should be part of the discussion when considering rent relief.

If you work for the tenant, you will want all this removed or mitigated.

We'll finish this section by noting that both the use clause and the restrictive covenant are directly linked in how they should be structured. If you inherit a poorly worded use clause and/or restrictive covenant, you should look for every opportunity to restructure each clause.

Chapter 15
TENANT BENEFIT CLAUSES™

A Tenant Benefit Clause is any clause in the lease that is solely beneficial to the tenant.

At first glance the tenant should say these are reasonable considerations in a supplier (landlord) customer (tenant) relationship. The rationale is that since the lease is favored to the landlord, it is reasonable to expect the tenant to negotiate clauses into the lease that benefit the tenant. In fact, anyone working for the tenant should vigorously negotiate for these types of clauses.

However, lets add to the definition: A tenant benefit clause is any clause in the lease that is solely and unilaterally beneficial to the tenant; thereby transferring _all the risk_ related to the item in the clause to the Landlord.

Overall, a well constructed lease, from the landlord's point of view provides a balance of risk between the parties and across the property. Tenant benefit clauses don't do this because the point of the clause is to eliminate the tenant's risk in a certain area of the operation of the property and/or the tenant's own business.

So what are the different types of Tenant Benefit Clauses?

Here are a few of the most common:
- A restrictive or exclusive use covenant,
- A co-tenancy clause,
- An option to terminate,
- An option to go dark or cease operations,
- Limits on the Landlord's ability to lease without benefiting the tenant, such as a "most favored" clause, and
- Renewal options.

There is a difference between tenant benefit clauses and clauses we call Trap Door ™ clauses, with the latter being clauses that on casual reading give the impression of one thing, but can also be interpreted a different way. Trap door clauses are intended to trip up the unsuspecting. Trapped Door clauses should never be drafted into the lease.

172

The party with the negotiating power will dictate if tenant benefit clauses are placed, or remain, on the table. When considering these clauses, the landlord must use their judgment to determine the amount of risk they want to assume to conclude the transaction.

However, for the landlord's team there are two very important considerations to negotiating all tenant benefit clauses.

1. Mitigating Overall Risk
2. Re-trading Risk Between the Parties

Mitigating Overall Risk
Some tenant benefit clauses can produce a compounding and cascading effect against the landlord, such as having a number of overlapping co-tenancy, termination or go dark clauses. This can work to the tenant's benefit. The landlord on the other hand needs to carefully consider if granting the clause will cause unintended consequences, and negotiate to remove or minimize those issues. This is why Tenant Benefit Clauses need to be abstracted from the lease. The leasing agent, or asset manager should request from the lease administrator a list of all other leases containing the same clause (ie: a co-tenancy clause) to determine if it could cause a compounding or cascading effect at the property. Careful drafting of the

clauses is also important to the landlord so the impact of the transferred risk is defined as narrowly as possible. For example, an exclusive use clause needs to be narrowly defined so the landlord retains as much control as possible for the merchandising and leasing of the property. Conversely, the whole idea of a TBC is to protect the tenant's interests and should be as widely worded as possible, if working for the tenant.

Re-trading Risk
Any time a tenant requests a Tenant Benefit Clause, it should be recognized that the risk has been transferred only to the landlord. Therefore, if the landlord is inclined to accept the concept of the tenant's request for the clause, the landlord may attempt to negotiate any or all of the following:
- placing conditions on the enactment of the tenant benefit clause, such as thresholds, timing, cure periods, etc.,
- limit the consequences if the clause is enacted,
- re-introduce clauses/ concepts the landlord previously agreed to step-downs or deletions to,
- obtaining a monetary consideration via an increase in the basic rent, or
- trading one tenant benefit clause for another, if there are requests for more than one.

174

Here is a further look at some of the more common tenant benefit clauses.

Co-Tenancy Clauses

There are essentially two types of co-tenancy clauses. The first is a co-tenancy clause tied to the opening or re-opening of the development or expansion, re-merchandising, etc. The second type of co-tenancy clause is related to the on-going occupation of the property by either types of merchandise, named tenants, or overall occupancy or a combination of these.

Opening Co-Tenancy

The tenant obviously wants some form of assurance that the project will be successful. As a result, the tenant may want to know that the anchor tenant(s) will open on-time and may also tie in other tenants either by name, style or an overall percentage.

In granting the clause the landlord should only agree to those items in their direct control. For example, the landlord should agree to a number of leases or area leased, not open. The reason is that the landlord can use reasonable efforts to ensure the tenant opens on a specific date, but it is typically only in the tenant's power to dictate the premises construction schedule, the arrival of inventory, receipt of permits, etc. The landlord shouldn't assume risk for those things beyond its direct control. The actual leasing of the property is within the control of the landlord.

The other issue with tying the clause to 'stores open,' is that the landlord can inadvertently create their own issue. This can happen if, as a result of the property not meeting the 'opening requirement', the tenant can also delay it's own opening. In effect, it creates a circular reference. And it happens, unfortunately.

If you are working for the landlord the consequence of the landlord not meeting the opening co-tenancy requirement should be limited to a monetary concession rather than a delayed opening or termination; and it should be limited to a temporary adjustment to the basic rent only. Operating costs and tenant specific charges should still apply because the related expenses will be incurred notwithstanding.

The landlord should also refrain from any co-tenancy that names specific tenants by name (either their legal corporate name or their trade name). There are many reasons for this.

The landlord may also limit the time of the reduced rent either using a period of time as a maximum or unless some other trigger is met, such as a certain sales volume. The tenant should object to this because it is contrary to the reason for asking for the clause in the first place.

In a phased development or a partial redevelopment, the question is if the co-tenancy should only apply to the specific phase or area of the development rather than the entire project becomes one of importance. The obvious reason for this is that the landlord doesn't want to inadvertently create an on-going co-tenancy or set up a punitive situation. For example, if the tenant is in an early stage of the a multi-phase development with that early stage ultimately constituting 45% of the entire project, the landlord doesn't want to agree to a 75% occupancy of the entire project rather than 75% of the specific phase. A reasonable tenant should accept this knowing that you are going into an earlier phase.

Fortunately, an opening co-tenancy has relatively limited impact over the life of the property as it is somewhat fixed in time around the opening of the project. The landlord should take care drafting the clause however, so as not to inadvertently create a perpetual co-tenancy requirement.

Here is a real world example. The tenant, a large drug store, was the anchor tenant for a new development. The wording in the opening co-tenancy clause gave the tenant the ability to do <u>any of the following</u> if the co-tenancy requirement was not met:

1. Reduce the minimum rent by 50%,
2. Not operate the store (a "Go Dark" clause) until the co-tenancy requirement was met. Ostensibly, the wording seemed to protect the tenant from opening immediately after construction was complete if the co-tenancy was not met, and
3. Terminate the lease.

The tenant wasn't obligated to pick one of the three; but could enact them together or sequentially due to the way the clause was worded. For example, the tenant could choose to go dark and not open and reduce the rent by 50% at the same time.

The landlord/developer was obligated to use 'best efforts' secure leases with both a medical clinic and a medical lab. Notwithstanding a vigorous leasing campaign aimed at attracting those specific uses, the property opened without the co-tenancy requirements in place.

The anchor tenant maintained that the clause simply stated that those uses were to be secured and since there wasn't a timeline for those deals to be completed prior to opening, the tenant interpreted the clause to be both an opening and continuous operating co-tenancy clause.

This is a major concern for that landlord as most leases in that landlord's property also contain ongoing co-tenancy clauses relative to the anchor space. This anchor effectively controls the investment in the property due to the co-tenancy clause wording.

While there may be legal room to argue the fine points of the clause in court, the process will be expensive and an outcome in the landlord's favor is not assured.

On-Going Co-Tenancy
A tenant in a new or established property may also request a co-tenancy provision for the entire term of their lease. The argument is the same as for an opening co-tenancy – the tenant is relying on the success of the overall property.

Again, the tenant may request that the provision be tied to certain tenants being in the property, a certain percentage of the property being leased (and open), etc.

The landlord, however, needs to carefully review any provision that spans several years. In addition to the same considerations required for an opening co-tenancy, here are some other things the landlord may negotiate.

If the landlord agrees to provide a co-tenancy, it may be time limited. For example it may only be effective during the first three years of the term while the tenant becomes established. A tenant should reject this, on the other hand.

The landlord should carefully consider both the historic vacancy at the property and the anticipated lease expires that coincide with the requesting tenant's term – or the time limit. This allows the landlord to negotiate from a position of knowing its potential risk to granting the provision. This is an example of the importance of good lease administration and a robust lease administration software that could provide a number of lease expiration reports based on area, percentage of gross leasable area and by each tenant by name.

Likewise, the landlord should look to see if granting the co-tenancy sets up a cascading effect with co-tenancy provisions in other leases as was the example with the drug store.

The co-tenancy clause should reasonably exclude vacancy caused by store closures due to renovations and relocations.

In a multi-phase and/or a multi-building development it is important for the landlord to limit the area to which the co-tenancy applies. Likewise, it is important to exclude the damage and destruction provisions from triggering the co-tenancy. However, as a tenant you want to avoid this as there are clauses in the lease pertaining to damage and destruction and the options the tenant should have.

Here is a real life example. In 2013 an arson fire completely destroyed a building in a 96% occupied, five building complex. The affected building housed approximately 20% of the tenants by number and area.

Other tenants in the property had co-tenancy agreements that permitted them to reduce their rent or terminate their leases if the total occupancy fell to less than 85%, by number or area. While the landlord's insurance provisions covered loss of income from the destroyed building, it did not include consequential revenue loss due to the business decisions to provide the other tenants with co-tenancy clauses.

Although some tenants attempted to rely on the 85% co-tenancy provision and reduce their rent; the leases excluded the fire from triggering the co-tenancy clause and the landlord's income was protected.

The landlord may also attempt to limit the tenant's ability to enact the provision to an actual and demonstrable reduction in the tenant's sales as a direct result of the loss of the co-tenancy. Again, a tenant should avoid this.

Options to Terminate or Cease Operations
These types of options are different than a co-tenancy only inasmuch as the tenant's ability to exercise the option is tied to something other than a certain percentage of the property being leased, or certain tenants being in the property. An option to terminate or cease operations is akin to a "get out of jail" free card in Monopoly®.

This type of clause, if broadly worded, gives the tenant ultimate control and the landlord assumes 100% of the risk without any control.

Even if the landlord conditions the exercising of either of these two different options with certain events – such as sales performance – the landlord has no direct control over the events leading to the exercise. For example, a store can manipulate its inventory to achieve a reduction in volume in order to exercise the clause, if the clause is tied to a minimum sales performance.

Landlords should object to these types of clauses arguing that the point of the lease is positive and proactive. The parties should not be contemplating 'what if' options. Smart merchants will still demand the option.

If the landlord does have to provide either an option to terminate or an option to cease operations, the landlord must mitigate the financial and business risks in the following manner:

Option to Terminate
Aside from placing conditions on when a tenant may exercise the option, such as a minimum sales volume, only after X number of years of the term, the death of the principle owner (in the case of a single owner specialty operation); the landlord will want significant notice before the lease is terminated to allow the landlord to find a replacement tenant.

The landlord also wants repayment of the unamortized portion of any inducements paid since they were provided in anticipation of the successful completion of the lease as well as the unamortized portion of any costs incurred in the leasing (including commissions and legal costs).

If the landlord incurs any costs requested by the tenant in the build-out of the space at the onset of the lease, these should be recaptured, if possible.

The landlord may want any other beneficial clauses, such as an exclusivity or restrictive covenant to end at the time of the notice. The reason for this is that the landlord may end up replacing the outgoing tenant with another like tenant. However, the landlord shouldn't assume that it will be in the same location or only occur once the departing tenant has left. Once the departing tenant has made it known they no longer want a relationship with this location, the landlord must concern themselves with the longer term impact on their property. It is important that this concept of the termination of these types of clauses occur before the end of the lease is clearly spelled out in the clause. It is rarely captured in the drafting of these clauses.

Option to Cease Operations

This is also known as a "Go Dark" clause. Landlords tend to favor this type of clause over an option to terminate since the landlord still receives an income steam. This clause allows the tenant to cease operations but still enjoy the lease and the space.

A dark premises in the property can be detrimental to the image and leasing of the property. It can also hurt other tenant's sales. Therefore, in addition to the conditions for an option to terminate; the landlord will want the option to terminate the lease at any time after the tenant has provided notice that it will cease operations. This allows the landlord to re-lease the premises, turn the lights back on and have an operating premises in addition to obtaining the rent.

Most Favored Clause
This is a term many have not heard before because it is our term for a new type of clause requested by knowledgeable, brand name tenants.

The concept of a most favored clause, as portrayed by the tenant, is that the owner won't act negatively to the tenant as compared to other tenants. The tenant's lawyer will submit broad wording that upon closer examination, shows its true intent. This intent means that the landlord won't negotiate any clauses contained in the tenant's lease on more favorable terms with any other tenant during the lease term. For example, if the tenant's lease has a three mile radius clause and the owner agrees to a two mile radius for another tenant, the original tenant radius will now be two miles.

Obviously, there are many significant issues with this type of clause. Essentially, the tenant who has this clause is perpetually in a position of negotiating their lease terms for the duration of the lease, plus they obtain the benefit of concessions that may only be available to a stronger tenant.

This type of clause also causes lease administration nightmares since the lease has the ability to constantly change.

If you work for the landlord be wary of all tenant submitted clauses that use words such as equitable, equally, etc. Pay particular attention to these clauses.

Tenant Benefit Clause Claw back
The landlord should always retain the ability to claw-back or terminate tenant benefit clauses if the tenant doesn't uphold its end of the contract. The lease document should contain specific wording that the tenant benefit clauses end if the tenant goes into default of the lease.

Likewise, the landlord needs to carefully review the lease for tenant benefit clauses should the tenant request any amendments to the lease, assignment or subletting. That is why all TBCs should be abstracted into the lease administration system. This allows the lease administrator to run reports on each type of tenant benefit clause and perform a lease risk assessment. Having the report in hand, the landlord can then introduce the termination of these clauses as part of those negotiations for amendments, assignments, etc.

188

Chapter 16
TRAP DOOR CLAUSES™

A trap door clause is any clause that can be read in more than one way. Typically, a trap door clause results from either a deliberate attempt to mislead the other party via ambiguous wording or context; or they arise from sloppy wordsmithing. The latter is due to either too much - or too little - verbiage and can be caught up in legalese.

Whether it is an attempt to mislead or bad lease crafting, trap door clauses rely on two basic negotiating elements:
1. both parties not being absolutely clear on the intent of the clause and the agreement between them; and
2. the party on the receiving, or granting, end of the clause assumes the meaning intended based on a preconceived notion or prejudice.

Here is a real life example of a trap door clause. Given the people involved, the reason for the clause being drafted into the in the lease in the manner described, the reason the trap door clause came to be was more than likely due to a combination of poor wordsmithing of the clause, interpreted by people involved in the property long after the initial negotiation and lease drafting, rather than a deliberate attempt to mislead the landlord. However, you can see how the issue arose as well as the consequences in this example.

The lease involved a sophisticated brand name tenant and an intelligent, experienced landlord. The clause pertained to the allocation of real estate taxes to the tenant premises and was drafted by the tenant, rather than the landlord, so it was 'off standard' to the landlord's lease form.

A paraphrase of the lease wording was that the tenant would pay as its portion of the total property taxes, those taxes applicable to the tenant's premises in proportion to the total tax bill and the taxes on the land under the tenant premises.

On the surface, this wording seems common and reasonable. To the landlord it seemed that the wording approximated the wording in their standard lease.

Other points to know and consider:
- The tenant's premises represented about 10% of the total GLA.
- The assessed value was based using the income approach.
- The municipality in which the property was located determined the property taxes based on the assessed value of the property and (arbitrarily) split the total tax bill between the land value and the value of the improvements on the basis of approximately 30% of the total bill was deemed to be on the land and 70% on the improvements.
- The tenant's per square foot rent was about 35% of the average rent in the balance of the property as they were a sub-anchor, and
- The building occupied about 25% of the total property area, with the balance being parking lot and landscaping.

How would you, as a Lease Administrator working for the landlord, determine the tenant's share of the taxes?

The landlord's lease administration department advised the accounting team to send the tenant a bill for 10% of the total taxes, as its proportionate share.

Since this chapter is about trap door clauses, you have already surmised that the tenant objected to the bill based on the wording in the lease. Here were their arguments:

- The lease provided that the tenant would pay its portion of those taxes applicable to the tenant's premises.

While the landlord read that to mean a proportionate share of the total tax bill (thus 10%), the tenant argued that since the tax bill was based on the assessed value of the property using the income approach, then it should be the tenant's rent assessment in proportion to the total tax. Since the tenant had a lower per square foot rent than the balance of the property, the value assessment on a per square foot basis was less than the balance of the property and far less than 10% of the total.

But that wasn't the tenant's only argument.

- Since the tax bill was separated into both land and improvements the tenant's portion above should be calculated only on the 70% of the overall tax bill (the improvements portion) as that represented the tenant's premises, and

- The land portion of the total tax bill should be based on a calculation of the tenant's premises area in the numerator and the total property land mass (including the parking lot and landscape) in the denominator. Their argument was that the lease specifically stated the tax on the land under the tenant's premises. Their interpretation of the clause included the unwritten word "ONLY". This had the effect of dramatically reducing the tenant's portion to almost 1/3 of the original tax bill.

Combined these created a significant shortfall to the landlord. Here is a simplified look at the effect of the landlord's billing v the tenant's calculation.

Landlord's bill: 10% of 100% of the bill

Tenant's interpretation of the clause:

Tenant's premises portion was 35% (their rent) of 10% (their area) of 70% of the total tax bill (representing the improvements portion of the tax bill) = 2.45% of the total applied to the improvements; plus

Tenant's portion of the land was $10/400^{1}$ X 30% of the total taxes = 0.75% of the total tax bill.

Tenant's interpretation of its total tax obligation, as a percentage of the total tax bill, was 3.2%.

Note[1]: 400 represents the tenant's premise area to the total land mass since the overall building occupied 1/4 of the total area of the property.

Quite a difference in cash flow between a 10% recovery and a 3.2% recovery.

Now lets take that one step further and look at the impact on value of that 6.8% slippage. At a 7% capitalization rate every dollar in slippage equates to $14.29 in lost value! That is almost $143,000 in value for every $10,000 the landlord didn't collect on the tax bill from this tenant.

In addition to the direct financial impact, the landlord and tenant had a strained relationship during to the discussions that followed, which included threats of court action by both parties.

For these obvious reasons we advise you to both be on the look out for trap door clauses as well as to never engage in putting trap door clauses into the lease. No one likes the idea of being hoodwinked and will remember it for a long time.

So what are the common trap door clauses?

The correct answer is; "It Depends."

Because trap door clauses occur by either sloppy lease drafting or by specific malicious intent, they can occur in any clause in the lease where the interpretation can differ from the language. A simple misplaced comma can have a significant impact.

The best way to protect the landlord or tenant is the old adage Say what you mean, mean what you say and then clearly, and concisely, write down the intent of the article EXACTLY as it should be read. If either party to the lease suspects the wording can be read in different ways, they should immediately point to the potential issue and demand clarification as to the meaning. That clarification should be specifically drafted into the lease.

Back to our example. The landlord and tenant eventually came to a mutual agreement on how the tax bill should be allocated to the tenant. That agreement resulted in a billing between the two interpretations. More importantly, the two parties also committed the revised agreement to paper by way of a lease amending agreement. If you discover a real or potential trap door clause, the clause should be discussed and the lease amended to eliminate future interpretation issues.

Chapter 17
STANDARD CLAUSES

BOILERPLATE

noun

☆ any of the standard clauses or sections of a legal document
  - Webster's

On balance the lease is generally divided into three sections (excluding schedules, exhibits and appendixes). Those are:

1. Proactive clauses. These include clauses concerning positive actions and includes the business terms of the transaction.
2. Negative Clauses. These include what happens if the positive actions do not occur, such as default provisions, bankruptcy, etc.
3. Standard legal or boilerplate clauses. These are clauses one expects to see from one lease to another.

In this chapter we will look at some of the 'standard' clauses that tenants negotiate, and how their typical step down requests to the standard wording may affect the landlord. This is not an exhaustive list, since every word in every lease is open for negotiation. Instead we will focus on some of the clauses that are negotiated most often that have the most impact on the landlord.

While this chapter is written specifically for landlords, tenants should read it carefully too because you can glean negotiating leverage by understanding the implications for the landlord.

These are:
- Reasonableness
- Mutual indemnity
- Self insurance
- Damage and destruction
- Default Provisions

Reasonableness
A fairly common request by tenants is that the landlord act reasonably in all it actions relative to the lease. While the landlord intends to generally act in a reasonable manner, the lease does provide areas where the landlord may be unreasonable and arbitrary. While this is more of a legal test, and you should consult your attorney

concerning the various tests and consequences of being, and proving being, 'reasonable', it does have business consequences and assumed risks.

The best solution for the landlord is to never grant a carte blanche agreement to act reasonably in all circumstances. In the alternative, ask the tenant why they are requesting the clause and to provide examples, then draft wording only into those clauses that you are comfortable with the concept.

Conversely, the tenant should always ask the landlord for a broad reasonableness clause.

Mutual or Reciprocal Indemnity
Another common request is that the landlord will indemnify the tenant, just as the landlord seeks an indemnity from the tenant. The request is almost always phrased this way too.

The issue is that the landlord is assuming a much greater implied and financial risk than the indemnity provided by the tenant, so it really isn't reciprocal or mutual.

Most leases provide that the tenant will indemnify and hold harmless the landlord for the actions of the tenant, and certain others, <u>within the tenant's premises or in the conduct of the tenant's business.</u> Therein is the problem, the tenant's premises is contained and within the tenant's control.

Conversely, the landlord has to contend with the balance of the property, with free access to the public in many types of buildings, such as retail shopping centers. The tenant is asking the landlord to assume disproportionate risk, given the scope of the difference in size of the area and the amount of control each party has over that area.

Depending on how the mutual indemnification clause is worded, it can also be deemed a trap door clause (see the chapter on trap door clauses for more information about these) because the tenant could argue that the cost of insurance for the common area and insurance deductibles don't apply to them due to the concept of indemnification by the landlord.

The best counter for the landlord to this type request is to deny it, point to the disparity and note that both parties carry insurance.

Self Insurance
A large, brand name tenant may request self insurance on some or all the items it is required to insure. Self insurance is where the tenant assumes all the financial risk for

a casualty. A simple example of self insurance may be where the tenant pays out of pocket for the replacement a broken glass door or window, rather than having plate glass insurance.

Aside from the example (because the cost is relatively minor), self insurance is fraught with problems, but the landlord may permit it to complete the transaction. Here are the potential pitfalls and potential solutions from the landlord's perspective.

Typically, the landlord wants to be named on the tenant's insurance, and as evidence of the coverage the landlord obtains a certificate of insurance from the tenant's insurance company. If the tenant is self insuring, the landlord needs to ensure that the lease wording is expanded to include that the landlord is still covered under the self insurance and that the tenant will provide separate acknowledgement of that concept.

Another pitfall is if the lease is assigned to another company. The assignee may not have the financial depth to pay out on a self insured claim. This may include an assignment to a subsidiary of the original tenant. The insurance section of the lease is often overlooked when considering assignments, and a good lease administrator should bring this clause up to the person(s) on the landlord's team considering an assignment. Bottom line is the landlord will incur additional management expense (and potential exposure) administering to the tenant's self insurance. The landlord should include a check of the insurance provisions in the lease if an assignment is contemplated and revert to the standard lease wording as a condition of the landlord's consent to the assignment, if needed.

If the tenant incurs several significant self insurance claims it may not have the ability to pay a claim. Likewise, the net worth of the tenant may suffer at some point for some other reason, such as the closure of a division, reorganization, liquidity issues, etc. The landlord's best defense in both these cases is to condition the tenant's ability to self insure on the value of the company being at least equal to the same amount at the start of the lease. Ideally, this should be stated numerically in the lease rather than just outlining the concept. Should the value of the tenant drop below a certain level then, the standard lease wording would apply and the tenant would need to insure through an insurance company.

And here is a big one.

Would allowing self insurance by a tenant be compatible with the provisions of the mortgage or the landlord's own insurance? Generally, speaking many lenders and insurance companies do not have an issue with limited self insurance provisions, such as self insurance on plate glass. It is important to know the obligations under both the mortgage and the insurance documents before negotiating or agreeing to self insurance provisions.

Damage and Destruction
The landlord can inadvertently assume more than the intended risk with modifications to these clauses. In addition, the landlord needs to be careful when crafting the property template lease – another reason not to accept an off the shelf lease form.

There are two scenarios when considering modifications to damage and destruction clauses. The first is damage to the tenant's premises. The second is damage to the balance of the property.

Damage to the tenant's own premises is pretty straight forward; however, the landlord should resist requests for a required relocation of the tenant's business, for a first right of refusal to release the rebuilt premises or to maintain the existing rent after reconstruction.

203

Since the tenant will negotiate this in the initial lease, the landlord would have to make a number of assumptions in granting any of these requests. For example, would the landlord have available space in the property for a required relocation? Will this be the right tenant in the right place after reconstruction? Will the space be rebuilt as is? What would be the net cost to the landlord for reconstruction and would the tenant's existing rent be appropriate at that time.

Damage to the property is a little different and depends on the type of development. A tenant may request the ability to terminate its lease or seek a substantial rent reduction for damage to the 'Property' as it is defined in the lease. However, that may not always be appropriate.

If, for example, the property is comprised of a number of buildings, one of those buildings may be destroyed with no affect on the tenant's business located in another building. Landlords want to avoid placing themselves in the position of the property emptying out when it is still viable as an operating concern.

Default Provisions

There are provisions in the lease for when agreements are not upheld. Many tenants automatically request adjustments to these as a matter of course. The adjustments most requested pertain to the time to cure a breach of the agreement.

The first inclination concerning these requests is to counter with a resounding "NO". After all, it is the tenant that has brought forward the breach; however, there are a number of reasonable explanations for a request for a longer time to cure a breach, particularly in a large company, so it is up to the landlord to determine the flexibility they want to offer.

For example, while rent is due on the first of the month in most leases, a rent payment may be mishandled by the postal service and arrive late even if the tenant sent it in a reasonable time frame before it was due. This type of breach is beyond the tenant's control, so the landlord may want to provide some leeway on providing notice. Please note that most jurisdictions around the world have laws to protect tenants from arbitrary forfeiture of their lease and the enjoyment of their space. As a result, the rules around those laws typically supersede what is in the lease.

There are a few types of breach that should never warrant a longer cure period than the landlord originally placed in the lease. The following types of breach should be excluded from any longer cure periods the landlord grants:

- Risk to the landlord's title in the property
- Risk to the landlord's insurance
- Risk to the landlord's mortgage
- Risk of personal injury or damage to others
- Environmental Risk
- Risk to the landlord's reputation
- Breach of authority or regulatory direction (ie: Health & Fire Department directions or Zoning bylaws)
- Any illegal activity

The risk to the landlord is substantially greater than the risk to the tenant for not having the additional cure period.

Chapter 18
ASSIGNMENTS AND SUBTENANCIES

Once an assignment or sublet is completed the landlord is no longer dealing with the person or entity they originally negotiated the lease with, so it is important to carefully consider the assignment and subleasing provisions at the time of the original lease negotiation.

This chapter has been written from the perspective of the landlord's position. If you are a lease administrator for a tenant you may find it useful to understand the landlord's perspective. However, there are certain aspects to your view as the tenant that will also be covered at the end of the chapter. Please don't be tempted to skip to that part.

Two caveats to the first paragraph. Although the original tenant is still the responsible party in a sublease (also called a sublet) situation, the daily operation of the business is in the hands of someone else. Therefore, there is an extra party involved in the lease that must be considered.

Likewise, a franchise operation may result in either a sublet or assignment of the original lease. Special considerations are required to protect the landlord when leasing to a franchising tenant, which we will also review.

Assignment
Typically, the landlord needs to consent to any assignment because the act of the assignment means the tenant is changing. An assignment can arise from a number of situations. Each may bring a different nuance to how the landlord will negotiate its consent. The two important underlying concepts of an assignment are:

    a. the lease contract is being transferred from one party to another, and

    b. the original tenant (assignor) is putting forward an entity to 'step into the shoes' of the assignor.

Two pretty basic concepts, but with these come two implications.

The first is that the new tenant (assignee) receives the benefits of the previously negotiated lease contract. All the previous tenant's negotiating strength is transferred and the landlord has limited ability at the time of the assignment to insert more negotiating strength. So it is important to ensure the landlord retains the negotiating strength during the initial lease negotiations, when discussing this clause.

How is this done? The first step is to require that the landlord's written consent is needed. The tenant may counter that the landlord's consent can't be unreasonably withheld. While it is always preferable to not provide this wording, if it is required then the landlord must spell out when withholding consent would be reasonable. The withholding of consent would be reasonable if it included, amongst other things, the assignee has a poor history, the financial covenant of the assignee is not to the landlord's standards, the reputation of the assignee is questionable, a trading in the landlord's real estate by assigning within a period immediately after commencement of the term or before the expiration of the term, a change in the rent structure, and if the assignor does not remain on the lease as an indemnifier or co-covenantor. The landlord needs to have wording in the assignment clause that allows the landlord to request information about the assignment and the assignee in order to assess the landlord's ability to provide consent. The specifics of what information is required is not drafted into the lease because that information may change over the term of the lease.

The next is to insert wording into all tenant benefit clauses that makes the clause personal to the original tenant, so the tenant benefit clauses can be removed at the time of an assignment.

The landlord should retain the ability to change the rent structure upon an assignment. There are many reasons for this. The tenant risk profile may be changing. The landlord and tenant now have a history that the assignee will benefit from, whereas in the original lease this may not have been known. If the original tenant a retailer and was paying percentage rent, the assignee may not generate the same sales and end up paying percentage rent. The landlord will want to protect this percentage rent income. And the natural lapse of time may warrant an increase in the same manner as a renewal option warrants an increase due to inflation.

A carefully crafted Use Clause is also beneficial during an assignment, because the assignee should conduct the exact same business as the original tenant in a retail property. Although typically not as important in an office or warehouse property, it is always a good idea to retain the tenant continuity during an assignment. If the new tenant requests a change in the use or an expansion in the use, the landlord gains negotiating strength because the assignor and assignee are both requesting a modification to the original agreement. This 'opens' the lease to further negotiation by the landlord, or the landlord may also simply say the lease is the lease and there is no option to change the lease at the time of the assignment.

The second implication of the assignment is that the risk associated with the original transaction has changed simply because the covenant of the operating tenant has changed. Granted it could be improved in a case where a small tenant wants to assign the lease to a brand name operator, for example; but this rarely happens.

The assignor is telling the landlord that the entity taking over the lease is as good or better than they are as a tenant. More often than not however, the assignee is an entity the landlord knows nothing or very little about. As a result, the landlord must protect themselves during the initial lease negotiation, with the original tenant, for a change in the risk profile associated with an assignment.

The best way to accomplish this is to secure additional comfort regarding the covenant as a condition of an assignment. The two preferred methods are to have the assignee provide a covenantor's agreement and/or a letter of credit; and have the assignor continue to indemnify and co-covenant the assignee.

Of course the landlord can also carry the ultimate big stick and have a standard clause in the lease that permits the landlord to terminate the lease if the tenant wants to assign it. As you can imagine, this type of clause is not popular with tenants. Those with significant leasing strength simple delete it, while others state that the landlord can't act to terminate the lease if the tenant withdraws the assignment request.

Why would an landlord want this type of termination ability in the assignment clause?

The philosophical reason is that the lease negotiated is personal to the tenant, as we discussed. If the tenant wants to interject another (typically unknown) party into the lease, then the landlord should be free to negotiate freely with the other party or any other party simply because it is the landlord's property and the landlord should retain control over whom they decide to do business with, rather than the tenant.

The more practical reasons are:

- The assignment may be the result of the tenant wanting out of a bad situation by selling to an unwitting or misguided entity. If the landlord allowed the assignment, then the landlord may be perpetuating a bad situation. It may be a tough recognition by all parties that the specific merchandising or use concept simply does not work at that property.
- The clause protects the landlord in case of an unauthorized assignment of the lease, that the landlord has not consented to in the first place. It gives back control of the premises to the landlord. The mere presence of the option to terminate in case of an assignment - requested or not – is also intended to put the tenant parties on notice that there is a potential and sizable risk to the business and tenancy if there is an unauthorized assignment.
- The assignment may also be a condition of a refinancing wherein the lease is pledged as security for the loan. This gives the lender control over the lease. Because loans tend to have preferred debtor rights under various

bankruptcy laws, the landlord may not want to lessen its rights in its real estate and elect to terminate the lease instead.

Large Corporation Assignments
Brand name tenants regularly request an amendment to the assignment clause wherein the landlord's consent is <u>not</u> required for an assignment of the lease to certain entities. Generally speaking these assignments are related to either the corporate structure of the company, such as an assignment of the lease to an affiliate or subsidiary of the tenant or as a result of corporate restructuring or financing. They can also relate to a share sale or an asset sale.

The landlord must be aware that each of these can mean the covenant of the tenant changes, sometimes dramatically. Here are a few examples:

A Sale

A national business with a superb covenant wishes to sell a few of it's locations and has found a buyer of the one location in the landlord's property. The covenant changes from a credit tenant to an independent tenant as a result. This can also trigger co-tenancy agreements, producing a cascading

214

effect on the property. To mitigate this risk, the landlord should insist on providing its consent to an assignment even if only a few of the tenant's locations are sold.

We also suggest that an assignment to another party without landlord's consent be for as wide a geographic area as possible (ie: all the locations in [named country, states, provinces, jurisdictions] are sold to a single entity), or a majority of the locations, including the landlord's location are sold to a single entity.

Did you also note the nuances in the general concepts?

It is important to note that the buyer is a single entity, otherwise the wording is meaningless because it could still permit a single unit sale. For the same reason, if using the concept of a majority of locations sold, the landlord's location must be one of those locations. Otherwise, the majority of all locations could be sold to one group and the landlord's specific location sold either individually or as part of a sale of a much smaller number of locations. The absence of the reference to the landlord's location as part of the majority sale defeats the protection the landlord wants.

A Re-Organization

The brand name tenant assigns the lease to an affiliate or subsidiary as part of a reorganization. Your lawyer will tell you that you have a new legal entity as a tenant. Thus, the covenant has changed. In some cases the tenant may have created an entity with the only purpose to hold leases. As a result, it only holds liabilities and no assets resulting in virtually no covenant for the landlord. To mitigate this risk, the landlord should insist on two things:

1. that any assignment encompass a majority of the leases to a single related entity. This protects the landlord in case the parent company spins off the subsidiary or affiliate, and

2. that the original or parent company remain as a covenantor after the assignment. This protects the landlord from an assignment to a shell or liability only company.

A Change in the Nature of the Business

A regional brand name tenant intends to grow its business by franchising it's concept. While the brand name remains, the covenant changes after the assignment, from the company and franchisor to the covenant of a franchisee. To protect itself the landlord should never include any type of assignment to a franchisee or licensee that can be completed **without** landlord's consent.

Later in this chapter we discuss the special considerations regarding franchises.

Now lets look at subleases generally.

Subleasing
In a sublease the original tenant is still the responsible party and is the actual tenant; however, the daily operation is conducted by someone else. Therefore, there is an extra party involved in the lease that the landlord must consider.

From the perspective of the initial lease negotiation, the landlord's consent should be required in the same manner as an assignment and the lease wording in the clause will generally include both assignment and subletting together. As a result, most of the comments about assignments apply to subleasing with a few notable exceptions.

The landlord's ability to terminate the lease, change the rent or claw back tenant benefit clauses is removed since the actual tenant under the lease (also known as the 'sublessor' or 'sublandlord' in a subletting situation) is not changing.

Conversely, the landlord doesn't want the tenant to 'trade in its real estate.' Too often landlord's leases are silent on whether or not the tenant can charge the subtenant more rent than the tenant pays the landlord. Some landlords agree to split any incremental rent the tenant receives 50/50. Neither concept seems satisfactory because the tenant is profiting from the landlord's (limited) stock in trade. The landlord should prohibit any type of incremental rent accruing to the tenant.

There are important items that should be discussed at the time of the request to sublease.

Your lawyer may tell you that to be a sublease rather than a de facto assignment, the tenant (sublessor) must reserve a part of the lease to itself. This can be a part of the rent, a part of the premises or part of the term. The most common way to deal with this legal provision, with the least amount of administrative or managerial time and cost, is to make the sublease match the (applicable) term of the lease less one day. This applies to the initial term and during any subsequent renewal periods.

This also means the sublease must be renewed each time the head lease is renewed. We advocate using a new sublease between the sublessor and the subtenant, and sublease consent between the landlord, sublessor and subtenant each time the head lease is renewed.

The landlord's consent document should include wording that states that accepting rent directly from the subtenant does not amount to an assignment of the lease to the subtenant, nor does it preclude the landlord from seeking any unpaid balance from the tenant. Since this must be very precise wording relative to the laws in your jurisdiction, it is important to have your lawyer construct the appropriate wording.

Franchises
A franchise organization presents unique dynamics to the leasing process. Not the least of which is determining who will actually be the tenant.

Some franchise organizations want to control the space and become the tenant. The franchisor enters into the lease and becomes the tenant, subsequently subleasing to the franchisee. Others prefer to provide real estate advice and services to the franchisee, such as site selection and lease negotiation, but the franchisee itself becomes the tenant. Knowing which concept will be used dictates the negotiating strategy of the landlord and how the lease is administered.

Franchisor as Tenant

This can seem like it is the most advantageous of the two options. However, it is important to carefully determine the covenant of the actual entity that will be the tenant. Many franchisors legally partition their business into different entities with royalty fee into one entity and leases held in another entity with no actual assets. It is important at the outset to have the franchisor clarify and prove the covenant of the true lessee and, if needed the landlord needs to introduce protections to the covenant such as an indemnification by the parent company, etc.

It is also a prudent business move not to let the franchisor assign all the responsibility of paying the rent to the franchisee. The franchisor typically has greater financial resources than the single franchisee.

Most franchisors will request that the landlord's consent requirement is waived for a bona fide franchisee as a subtenant. This is fairly common and is acceptable since the franchisee is vetted in the franchising process and the franchisor remains on the lease as the tenant. However, be careful of wording that includes a "sublease or assignment" since these are two different concepts, as we have discussed.

220

When negotiating the initial lease, the franchisor may condition the offer to lease to securing a franchisee within a certain timeframe. The common request is for a 90 day period to find a franchisee. This is also common, but if the landlord agrees to this, the landlord must retain the ability to potentially lease the space to others while the franchisor is attempting to find a franchisee. This clause is often negotiated so that if the landlord finds an alternate tenant (subject to vacant possession), the tenant has a very limited time to waive its condition, such as 48 hours. This type of compromise wording meets the business objectives of both the landlord and the franchisor.

Franchisee as Tenant
This is becoming more common if the franchisor doesn't want to assume the liability of the costs of the lease.

A franchisor may enter into an offer or lease with an added proviso that it can be assigned to a bona fide franchisee of the system without triggering the landlord's options to increase the rent, terminate, charge an administration fee, etc.

Don't Make This Real Life Mistake
Unfortunately, we've seen instances where the tenant is listed in the offer to lease as "to

be named" or "a franchisee of XYZ brand". Our lawyers advise us that because one of the two parties to the contract cannot be specifically identified, there is no valid contract. Your lawyer will probably say the same, so insist on having the franchisor named on the offer and/or the lease. The change in the tenant can always be dealt with in the consent to assignment document.

Alternatively to the franchisor securing the space, the franchisee may find the location, start the negotiation and then turn over the final lease negotiation to the franchisor's real estate department; however, the franchise becomes the tenant.

In either case, the covenant the landlord has is with the franchisee and not the franchisor so the landlord must go through their normal vetting process when leasing and secure the covenant with a covenantor's agreement, letter of credit, etc.

A unique dynamic when the franchisee is the tenant is that the landlord gains a brand name tenant; but the control of that brand rests with a third party who is not part of the operating agreement between the landlord and the tenant/franchisee. While this is not a concern where the franchisor is the tenant, and is part of the agreement with the landlord; it does have implications in this case.

Consider the answer to this question. What happens if the tenant loses the franchise? No landlord wants the internationally known burger franchise they negotiated for to become a single location hamburger stand almost overnight.

The implication for the former franchisee can be financially fatal if the former franchisee is required to remove marks, design elements, colours, menus, etc. identifiable to the franchisor and then reconstruct and rebrand as something else. As a result, the landlord will also likely lose a tenant. Moreover, it could have little or nothing to do with the landlord's property because the loss of the franchise agreement may stem from some other aspect of that business arrangement between the franchisee and the franchisor. This too can trigger cascading co-tenancy issues in other leases.

Because the franchise agreement is a third party agreement, the landlord has little recourse in this situation. In fact, because the tenant will continue to be the former franchisee and retains a right to occupy the premises, the landlord and franchisor are both precluded from entering into another lease for that space. This has been the case where the location has been successful but animosity has built between the franchisee and the franchisor.

The best protection for the landlord is to condition the continued tenancy on the tenant being a bona fide franchisee of that specific system. If the tenant loses the franchise, then the landlord can terminate the lease on short notice.

While this may seem like an end game solution where the landlord loses the rent because the landlord terminates the lease, it is no worse a situation than they may likely face. The cost of un-banding, closing for renovations and creating a new business may force the tenant out of business over time with the possibility of a replacement tenant lost. Or the landlord is stuck with a tenant that may not have a brand that contributes to the property as a whole; and yet, the tenant may also enjoy all the negotiating strength and privileges the brand name tenants could secure in the negotiation (ie: exclusivity, etc.).

More recently, the industry has seen a hybrid of the two types of franchise tenants.

In this case the franchisee is the tenant, but the franchisor retains some control over the space. This is done in the assignment section of the tenant/franchisee's lease and is sometimes referred to as a franchisor's reversionary option.

Here is how the option works.

The tenant is in default of the lease and the landlord notifies the franchisee that it is in breach. The landlord concurrently notifies the franchisor of the breach. The franchisor retains the option to cure the breach and if the franchisor does so, the lease is immediately assigned to the franchisor. The defaulted franchisee is out of the premises and the franchisor becomes the tenant. The franchisor also simultaneously reserves the right to assign the lease, now in the name of the franchisor, to a new bona fide franchisee of the system with such lease still containing the franchisor's reversionary option.

The key elements of granting a franchisor's reversionary option are to keep the franchisor's timeframe to cure the breach the same as contained in the franchisee's lease so any issues don't compound, and not to condition the franchisor to have a replacement franchisee to any period of time, otherwise the franchisor could potentially close the business during the period while they seek a new franchisee/tenant. The landlord wants the breach cured immediately and wants the public to have a seamless experience at the franchise without any undue downtime during the transition.

This type of reversionary option is as close as the landlord may get to having the franchisor as the actual tenant throughout the term. For that reason, we advise our clients to include a reversionary option in the negotiations where the tenant is the franchisee, even if it is not suggested by the franchisor.

One last word of caution about leasing to a franchise system, irrespective of who the tenant is on the lease.

The landlord should never permit a step down in the lease that allows the tenant to remove its improvements *at its option.* Franchisors build their brand through identification, as well as other things. Trademarks, copyrights and patents, in some cases, protect many design components to the premises. Leaving those improvements in situ does not mean that those rights and protections vest to the landlord or a subsequent tenant.

One unfortunate landlord found this out the hard way when an iconic, free standing building that was purpose built for the fast food tenant became vacant with all improvements, except the tenant's sign, left behind - at the tenant's option. The landlord found a replacement tenant. Shortly after the new tenant opened for business the former tenant demanded the new tenant and the landlord remove all identifiers to avoid consumer confusion, citing their design protections.

The end result was the design elements including the exterior wall finishes, roof line profile, etc. had to be removed and a new design installed. The cost to the landlord and the new tenant was significant in expense, management time and reputation.

The Tenant's Perspective

By now you will have gained an appreciate of where the landlord sits concerning assignments and subletting the premises. Intuitively, you may have also gained insights into how to improve your position as the tenant lease administrator. It would be too simple to leave it at that however.

An assignment is far easier to administer to than a sublease since the assignee is stepping into your shoes as the tenant, unless the assignor was obligated to indemnify or otherwise act as a covenanter the assignee or it was an internal assignment as part of a reorganization.

If it is an internal reorganization then its probable that there is no real change in lease administration scope or duties.

If it is the case that the assignor indemnified the assignee, then the tenant's lease administrator should create a file – preferably in the lease administration system – covering all items and conditions that may exist between the assignor and the assignee. However, this is rarely done, as once the assignment has been completed with the other party, both tend to go about their own business and trust nothing will go wrong. A knowledgeable tenant will, for example, insist on certain conditions with the assignee if they remain liable in any way for the lease, such as an annual financial and business review with the assignee. These types of conditions need to be recorded and a reminder system created otherwise the conditions are somewhat meaningless.

In the case of the tenant subleasing the space and becoming a sub-landlord, the lease administrator should recognize that the tenant has become both tenant with responsibilities to the landlord, and become a sub-landlord with a sub-tenancy responsible to the tenant.

In all likelihood there will be additional responsibilities, critical dates and events that must be managed between the three parties, with the tenant/sub-landlord acting as an intermediary. For example, aside from the obvious obligation of the sub-tenant to pay the rent there will also be a need to provide annual proof of insurance, an obligation to provide certain notices within time frames and to even audit the head landlord's invoices, annual rent notices and statement of operating costs.

There is also an obligation to keep basic information current, such as contact information for both the sub-landlord and the subtenant.

230

Chapter 19
ESTOPPELS

Why Estoppels?

A commercial real property lease is supported by a three-legged stool. One leg is the tenant; one is the landlord; and one is the lender. Without one of those legs, the stool won't serve its purpose.

Estoppel certificates or letters (and we'll describe them merely as "estoppels") may be bothersome or annoying, but they are needed to make or keep a healthy relationship among the three legs of the property business. Tenants need them when assigning their leases or when subletting space as well as when borrowing money against the lease. Landlords need them when selling the property or borrowing against the property. Lenders need them when lending against the property. All are legitimate purposes and all are contemplated when a lease is signed even if the lease doesn't say so (even though it should).

While it may be difficult at times to achieve them, harmonious relationships among all three legs are very worthwhile. Disputes should be limited to substantive matters, not be over cooperating with one another. If there is no other reason to strive to maintain a harmonious relationship, keep the following in mind: "Turnabout is fair play." There is no proper place for "revenge" in the estoppel process.

Furnishing estoppels is an administrative matter, not a substantive one. There may be items under dispute that will be covered by an estoppel, but responding to the request for the estoppel should not be one of them. And, it shouldn't matter whether the lease requires one party or the other to furnish one. Estoppels are needed to support the property, to keep the stool upright, so to speak.

Timing of Responses

Experience informs us that the most common tension as between landlords and tenants about estoppels is that the requesting party often has made its request too close in time to when the certificate is needed. Sometimes that situation is inevitable; sometimes it is the result of carelessness. Regardless of the reason, the need for a quick response frequently causes unneeded tension. It may seem that landlords are those most often pressuring their tenants for a quick turn-around. That's only because, by far, landlords request estoppels more frequently from tenants than tenants request them from their landlords.

Fundamentally, regardless of the reason the requesting party waited too long to make its request, landlord-tenant relationships should not be poisoned by a manufactured dispute based on how many days the lease might set for a response. Just because a lease says that a tenant (or a landlord) has 20 days to furnish an estoppel doesn't mean that it has to take 20 days. If the requesting party is in a crunch, it makes good sense for one leg of the stool, the tenant-leg or the landlord-leg, to hold up the stool. Basically, the golden rule is a good one to apply.

A Little Substantive Law

It's now time for some substantive "law." None of what follows is a substitute for actual legal advice. It is only general information to provide background to all readers.

What is the legal effect of an estoppel? "Estoppel" is a strange word. To understand its effect, try this non-defining, circular statement: "One who issues an estoppel certificate is then 'estopped.'" Basically, the certifying person (or entity) is "stopped" from denying that what is said in the certificate is a fact. If one issues an estoppel saying that the traffic light was red, those reasonably relying on that certificate can act as if the light was red even if it wasn't. In "leasing" terms, if a tenant delivers an estoppel in favor of a prospective successor landlord and that certificate says that the tenant has received all of the tenant improvement money due under the lease, the successor landlord can rely on that statement even if the tenant was mistaken. The tenant is "estopped" or "barred" from making a claim against the successor landlord for that money. The tenant, not the successor landlord, takes the risk of being wrong.

That's right, to be "estopped" means to be "barred" from asserting a fact or making a claim inconsistent with a previous taken position. In the case of an "estoppel certificate," the previously taken positions would be the statements in the certificate itself.

The obligation to deliver an estoppel is not imposed by law. It arises out of the contractual agreement. That means within the lease. So, the starting point to think about the estoppel is when the lease is being prepared. If a lease doesn't require one party or the other to deliver a certificate, it isn't a default to refuse to do so. It may not be appropriate to refuse or it may not be helpful (in the long run) to refuse, but it isn't a default under the lease.

If a lease requires one party or the other to deliver an estoppel (and, it is wise and appropriate that the requirement be mutual), but the lease is silent as to "how quickly," the "law" implies "within a reasonable time." Obviously, it is better that a lease set a time limit. Ten days would be at the short end, 30 days would reasonable, though a little bit of a stretch. Fifteen days seems about right, but for large enterprises, that might be a little bit "tight" for the bureaucracy to assemble the information needed to complete the certificate.

Examples of Lease Provisions

It isn't to anyone's advantage to have the lease provide merely that estoppels must be delivered to the requesting party within a given time period. A lease should describe what will or must be in the certificate. Here are sample clauses. These are not offered as exemplars to be used blindly, but only to show how such lease provisions might be written.

235

Tenant, without charge therefor, at any time and from time to time (but no more than twice in a calendar year), within 15 days after request therefor by Landlord or Lender, will execute, acknowledge, and deliver to Landlord a written estoppel certificate, in reasonable form, certifying to Landlord's designated mortgagee, other lender or any prospective purchaser of the Property, as of the date of such estoppel certificate, but only to the extent true: (i) that Tenant is in possession of the Premises and has unconditionally accepted the same; (ii) that this Lease is unmodified and in full force and effect (or if there has been any modification, that the same is in full force and effect as modified and setting forth such modifications); (iii) whether Tenant is aware of any then existing set-offs or defenses against the enforcement of any right or remedy of Landlord (and, if so, specifying the same in detail); (iv) that Rent is paid currently without any offset or defense thereto (or, if not, specifying the nature of any offset or defense in detail); (v) the dates, if any, to which any Rent has been paid in advance; (vi) whether Tenant is aware of an existing claim it holds of Landlord's default under this Lease and if so, specifying the same in detail; (vii) that Tenant has no knowledge of any event having occurred that authorizes the termination of this Lease by Tenant (or if Tenant has such knowledge, specifying the same in detail); and (viii) any other matters relating to the status of this Lease that Landlord reasonably may request be confirmed, provided that such facts are accurate and ascertainable. Only persons and entities to which such written estoppel certificates are directly addressed will be entitled to rely upon them.

Landlord, without charge therefor, at any time and from time to time (but no more than twice in a calendar year), within 15 days after request therefor by Tenant or any leasehold lender, subtenant, prospective subtenant, assignee or prospective assignee, will execute, acknowledge, and deliver to Tenant a written estoppel certificate, in reasonable form, certifying to Tenant's designated leasehold mortgagee, assignee, prospective assignee, subtenant or prospective subtenant or any other person designated by Tenant, as of the date of such estoppel certificate, but only to the extent true: (i) that Landlord owns or is the sole ground tenant of the Property (stating which is the case); (ii) that this Lease is unmodified and in full force and effect (or if there has been any modification, that the same is in full force and effect as modified and setting forth such modifications); (iii) that Rent is paid currently (or, if not, specifying the amount and nature of any deficiency); (iv) the dates, if any, to which any Rent has been paid in advance; (v) whether Landlord is aware of an existing claim of Tenant's default under this Lease and if so, specifying the same in detail; (vi) that Landlord has no knowledge of any event having occurred that authorizes the termination of this Lease by Tenant (or if Landlord has such knowledge, specifying the same in detail); and (vii) any other matters relating to the status of this Lease that Tenant reasonably may request be confirmed, provided that such facts are accurate and ascertainable. Only persons and entities to which such written estoppel certificates are directly addressed shall be entitled to rely upon them.

There is no single formulation for an "estoppel certificate" provision in a lease. Many prefer that a lease include a form of estoppel as an exhibit. That makes good sense, though it is rarely seen. Organizations with a lot of leases should consider developing a standard, fair form of estoppel and try to have that attached to every lease. If successful, the lease file should contain a "red-lined" comparison copy of the actual lease exhibit to the standard company form. Reference to that comparison copy will guard against the person completing the estoppel "assuming" she or he already knows what information is being called for based on familiarity with the organization's own form.

Without doubt, accepting the obligation to furnish an estoppel is a burden and the benefit to the certificate giver isn't immediately apparent. Basically, it is part of the deal. It is just the cost of doing business. Reciprocity of the obligation may seem like "the benefit," but it has to be conceded that most tenants will never need or request one. On the other hand, very few lease obligations seem to have an immediate benefit. Paying rent is such an example. It would be nice not to be required to pay rent, but that (too) is part of the deal. So, don't gripe about the work it takes.

Caution!

If no other point has yet been brought home, keep this one in mind. The statements in an estoppel will be treated as true even if they weren't. So, it is important for there to be no light between what an estoppel statement says and the actual facts. For that and other good reasons, the task of preparing an estoppel should not be kicked around the office or given to the last name added to the payroll. The recipient of the certificate deserves a quality response. The giver, with a few clicks of the keyboard, is binding itself to its words. Just as with other important tasks, experience matters.

The Information Gathering Process

Some facts are easy to verify. One place to look is within the accounting or accounts payable department. Those departments have to have a culture to understand that furnishing this information is a part of their job just as is paying the bills. Has all the due and payable rent been paid as of the date of the certificate? That should be an easy one for an organized landlord or tenant. If either has difficulty in determining what has been paid or what should have been paid, then don't get angry at the need to furnish a certificate or the burden that supplying one imposes. Instead, reorganize your accounting procedures and records. Know how much rent is payable and know what is payable in the form of additional rent – taxes, operating expenses, insurance premiums, utility charges, merchants associations fees, and whatever else the lease might call for. Keep in mind those could just as easily be overpaid as can be underpaid.

Whether digital or physical, all correspondence and all memorandums concerning a particular leased space should be in one, readily accessible place. And, that's not only for the purpose of responding to requests for estoppels; it is for the primary purpose of managing the location. All matters concerning a particular leased space should be on file in a lease management file for that space. If that is done, and done religiously, the person responding to an estoppel request won't have to conjure up a list of every person or department in the organization who might "know something." While not directly applicable to the topic of "estoppel certificates," it would be a good organizational culture for everyone in the organization to memorialize all "potential" issues along with all developed issues. Obviously, reviewing such a central lease file must be done when preparing an estoppel.

Even if there is a central lease file, and obviously if there isn't, upon receipt of a request for an estoppel, the person responsible for preparing the certificate must reach out to others in the organization to inquire about any facts concerning disputes, defaults, potential defaults, and other items of importance. Every tenant and every landlord will be organized differently. So, the person or persons who are tasked with preparing estoppels need to understand their own organization. Possible sources of information are legal departments, lease administration departments, real estate departments, accounting departments, store management departments, and construction departments.

Regardless of whether an organization's "information giver" is in the same building, at a remote building, in the field or at the property, the person preparing the estoppel has got to tell that person the date by when their response is needed. And, that has to give them reasonable time to "get to it" and investigate. Sufficient time must be given to review the response and possibly to do further investigation. If an estoppel has to be furnished in 15 days, then answers need to be back in 5 to 7 days. Of course, depending on the size and structure of an organization, these time marks will change. And, make sure everyone involved in the process understands that while responding to requests for estoppel-related information is unrewarding, it is part of the "job."

There is only so far one can go with a "paper" search. The responder needs to reach out to field personnel. In the case of tenants, that means store managers, store maintenance supervisors, and district managers. For landlords, that means on-site personnel, off-site property managers, and maintenance supervisors. Keep in mind that the person responsible for preparing estoppels probably has a lot of experience in doing so; store managers or on-site property managers may never have done so before. Even if they have, their experience has to pale by comparison. For that reason, it is a good idea for every organization to prepare a checklist or at least a set of instructions for field people and include that checklist or set of instructions with every single request for information. The field people, just like those on the "home" staff, should see the actual questions or statements from the estoppel request. If a question or statement isn't obvious on its own (and few are), a paraphrased "interpretation" should also be sent. For example, most estoppels cover "defaults," but not everyone understands what could be a default. So, field (and often inside) people should be reminded that the certificate preparer wants to know such things as whether the landlord or tenant, as the case may be, is maintaining the property.

When polling people within an organization, the bottom line question should be: "Do you know of any problems or potential problems with the landlord or tenant (as the case maybe) or with the property or with other tenants?" Tell them that you want an expansive response and they shouldn't prejudge whether the potential or actual problem is serious. That's for the "company" to decide by way of having an experienced individual prepare the actual estoppel.

Field people often don't know about specific lease provisions. They often don't know about exclusive use rights or restrictions imposed on the landlord or tenant, as the case may be. For that reason, when an inquiry for information is sent to store managers, property managers or other field staff, copies of the relevant exclusive use right or restrictions against particular uses, and items of similar character, should be sent with the request for information. An important example might be that a store manager is completely unaware that other tenants are barred from selling certain goods even though those other tenants are actually doing so. If a tenant certifies that it knows of no defaults on its landlord's part when another tenant is actually violating that tenant's exclusive use rights, the certificate giver may very well be waiving a future claim. That would be an unpleasant result.

Similarly, if there are "no-build" areas or special maintenance obligations, such as the landlord's to repave the parking lot every five years, on-site personnel wouldn't know about them without being told. So, tell them at the same time as the question is asked.

The Trilogy: Represent, Warrant, and Covenant

Often, a requested estoppel form will recite: "Certifying party represents, warrants, and covenants that ...." These three terms do not have the same meaning. None of the "other" two words are there just to emphasize the third. We may always recite, "Larry, Moe, and Curly," as if they were co-joined triplets, but they aren't. The same is true for "represents, warrants, and covenants."

To "covenant" is to agree or promise. Instead of saying, "I covenant to do such and such," you could (should) say, "I agree to do such and such."

To "warrant" is to guaranty, essentially to agree to make good if something turns out not to be as stated.

To "represent," is to state that something is true and that the receiving party has the right to rely on the truth of what was said.

This trilogy ("represent" – "warrant" – "covenant") is thrown about so casually that it isn't possible to generalize as to what the cumulative effect might be. Try replacing the word "covenant" with the word "agree" and then reread the statement being requested as part of the estoppel. To "covenant" does not mean to "acknowledge." It means to "agree" in the sense of to "promise."

One way to appreciate the difference between making a representation and giving a warranty is to understand the consequence of each statement. In the case of a representation, the "relying" party may act as if the representation (statement) was true, but only if that relying party either did not know it was untrue at the time it was given or if the relying party couldn't have easily known it was untrue. That's what "reliance" is all about. In addition, in appropriate circumstances, though unlikely in an estoppel, if a material representation is untrue at the time given, the recipient of that representation may suspend its contractual obligations or even terminate an agreement with the representing party. For example, in the normal transaction, if a car seller represents that the car runs, and it doesn't, the buyer can terminate any agreement to buy that car because whether a car runs is material. Of course, if the buyer really knew that the car didn't run, it could not rely on the representation.

In contrast to a "representation," the falseness of which would allow a party to terminate an agreement or to claim damages if the recipient of the representation actually relied on it, the effect of someone "warranting" the truth of a statement is that the warranting party will have the opportunity to "make good" by fixing what was wrong. So, if our car seller warrants that the car runs, but didn't represent that the car runs, the seller will have the right to fix the car, thereby, in most cases, precluding the seller from terminating the purchase contract and even from claiming most kinds, if not all kinds, of damages.

To put that in real estate leasing terms, if a landlord represents that the HVAC works and it doesn't, its prospective tenant might have the right to terminate a lease before it begins (assuming the HVAC was material, such as for a data center, and that the representation wasn't in the form: "the HVAC will be in good working order on the Delivery Date"). It's more complicated than that, but the tenant would have greater rights than if the landlord had only warranted that the HVAC works. In the case of such a warranty, the tenant would have to accept delivery (if the lease were otherwise silent), even if the HVAC did not work, and the landlord would have the opportunity and obligation to put the HVAC in working order.

The distinctions between and among "represent," "warrant," and "covenant" are important because those terms almost always appear in an estoppel. Sometimes, the certificate will ask the respondent to "state." That's the functional equivalent of making a representation.

Representations, and possibly warranties, have a rightful place in an estoppel. Covenants do not. Either a party has already agreed to do something or to refrain from doing something or it hasn't. An estoppel is not the place to accept new obligations. Does that mean that the word "covenants" or words of similar import should be struck out on "principle"? Probably not. In most cases, using those words is harmless because, in the context presented, there is nothing actually being agreed-to by the certifying party. In other cases, all they serve to do is republish an existing promise or agreement. So, if it is valuable to maintain a harmonious relationship with the requesting party (or to keep the relationship from going further downhill), and it is harmless to say that a party "covenants," it is best to "let it go."

Warranting something that one has already obligated to warrant, such as where a tenant is already responsible to keep the HVAC in good, operating condition, is also harmless. If a tenant, in an estoppel, warrants that the HVAC is in good, operating, and the lease already places that obligation on the tenant, it doesn't add to the tenant's burdens. So, as with use of "covenant," the term "warrants" should only be stricken if it adds an obligation not already in existence.

Representations, however, are the heart and soul, the engine so to speak, of an estoppel. Even though the "breach" of a representation has the consequences already described, representations really serve two practical purposes. The first is what has already been discussed, to bind the "representer" to its word even if the facts were different. The other is as a due diligence or investigatory tool on the part of the requesting party. For example, if a tenant represents that its landlord in not in default of any obligations under the lease but for the landlord's failure to repair a roof leak, the tenant will be out of luck later claiming otherwise. That's true about the "no default" portion of the example. But, what about the part of the representation that said that the roof leaks?

The roof may or may not require repairs and if repairs are required, the landlord may or may not be the one obligated to make them. If the tenant reasonably believes that its landlord is in default of its obligations under the lease to repair the roof, then it is appropriate to say so in the tenant's estoppel. The tenant can't knowingly lie and it can't be recklessly indifferent as to the truth of the matter, but it can state what it reasonably believes. Does this mean that the tenant will be liable to the party relying on the certificate if the roof doesn't need repairs? No, the recipient "asked" the question about the landlord's possible defaults as part of its property investigation and is now alerted of a "possible" roof leak.

When listing "issues" in an estoppel being provided to a lender, it isn't fair to include trivial items that are "always" worked out in the normal course of business. Lenders don't understand that there are often "undone" items awaiting attention. Converting an estoppel that a landlord or a tenant, as the case may be, needs for a loan into a sledgehammer won't be helpful going forward. It might get the $200 worth of ceiling tiles replaced a little quicker, but at the cost of poisoning a long-term relationship. If, however, an estoppel is for a prospective buyer, assignee or subtenant, and the issue can't be worked out directly between the certificate giver and the certificate recipient, list the issue.

Weasel Words (Words of Qualification or Limitation)

Something needs to be said about "weasel words." They are necessary. What are they? For now, here's a single example: "Certifying party represents that to its knowledge, without any duty of investigation, such and such is true."

There are some items that the certifying party should stand behind without qualification (unless there is a real reason for doubt, in which case the doubt should be set forth in the certificate). For example, a landlord or tenant, as the case may be, should represent whether the rent is paid through a given date and not use any weasel words when giving such a representation. If, however, a tenant knows that it owes a tax reimbursement to the landlord, but the amount is in dispute, it should state that fact. If it holds the view that its rent is paid by virtue of a credit owed to it, it should state that fact. In those cases, it isn't appropriate to merely say: "Tenant is unaware that any rent is now due and owing to Landlord."

Similarly, a tenant or landlord should be obligated to know if it has "received" any notice from a governmental authority. Who else would know without polling every possible such authority? This is information in the hands of the responding landlord or tenant and not readily available elsewhere. On the other hand, it is inappropriate for a tenant or landlord, as the case may be, to be asked to represent that it is not in violation of any laws. That example invites an exposition on "weasel words," a concept dropped in above. "Weasel words" isn't a term used in the "law." The phrase's meaning is intuitive. Weasel words are words that qualify a statement. They aren't like crossing one's fingers behind one's back where they can't be seen. They are placed right up front. They are words of "qualification" and are commonly seen.

Perhaps tagging words of qualification as weasel words is a bit unfair, and not only to the weasel. In the example above dealing with whether a party is in compliance with all laws, certain qualifications are appropriate. First, there are too many "laws."

252

It is unreasonable to expect, let alone believe, that the certifying party even knows of every applicable law or whether it is in compliance. Such a representation, if it needs to be given, would appropriately be limited to "material" laws or all laws other than those, the violation of which would not have a material, adverse effect. It isn't unreasonable to expect that a party should know about laws that directly impact its business or whether it is in compliance with those important laws.

The "qualifier" of materiality goes to the laws themselves, but what about knowing if one is in compliance or not? In the end, that's a legal conclusion and estoppels are not legal opinion letters. They are about "facts." So, is it reasonable for the certifying party to know all of the relevant facts? Obviously, if a tenant or landlord knows of a violation of law, it shouldn't hide that knowledge. Otherwise, no. Words of qualification are to protect a party from being trapped by the "unknown," not to avoid telling the truth. Therefore, when giving an estoppel, known facts should be disclosed in the form of, "except as follows:" and then listing the exceptions. When a tenant wants to report a default by its landlord, such as a default in being reimbursed, it isn't appropriate to say merely, "Landlord is in default of its obligations under the Lease." That's not what was being asked no matter how the question was posed. The proper representation, before we proceed to write that it isn't, is: "Landlord is not default of its obligations under the Lease except that it has failed to reimburse Tenant in the amount of $35,000 on account of the Tenant Allowance."

The example last given is a stepping off point for some other common weasel words. Can a tenant (or for that matter, a landlord) be sure that its counterparty to the lease really isn't in default? No, it can't. The best that can be said is that is doesn't know otherwise unless it really, really "should" know otherwise. For example, the burden to determine if the rent has been paid to date is slight. Therefore, the certifying party should assume that burden. Similarly, a tenant should know if it has sublet the leased space, and should give the appropriate representation without reservation. Similarly, it should know if it has any right to extend the term of the lease or to buy the property beyond what is in the lease itself. There is no place for any "qualifying" modifier to such representations. On the other hand, the burden to investigate the violation or non-violation of every obligation that the other party may have in a lease can be overwhelming. For that reason, it would be legitimate to tell it like it is: "Here is what we actually know or are aware of."

Some of the examples above deal with "what the lease says." But, a lease should speak for itself. So, it is probably inappropriate for the requested estoppel to ask the certificate giver "what is in the lease," though many do just that. When faced with a request for a representation as to what the rent schedule looks like or whether there are any renewal rights, it would be appropriate to attach the lease and make the representation refer to the lease. Of course, it is proper to make an unqualified representation as to whether the lease has been modified because a party to a lease "should" know that and an outsider relying on the estoppel would not.

Another appropriate form of response is as follows: "<u>Except as expressly set forth in the Lease</u>, Tenant has no options to renew or extend the term of the Lease, no right of first offer or right of first refusal to lease or occupy any other space within the Leased Premises, and no right to cancel or reduce the term of the Lease. <u>Notwithstanding the foregoing</u>, Tenant has a first right to lease adjoining space contiguous to the Leased Premises pursuant to Article XX of the Lease."

If forced (or if it is convenient) to make statements as to what the lease "says," then it is appropriate to add the following to an estoppel: "In the event of any difference between the provisions of this Certificate and those of the attached Lease, the provisions of the attached Lease will prevail." Basically, as will be emphasized later, an estoppel should stick to its purpose, and not be a means of amending a lease.

The certificate giver will be, and should be, charged with knowing the contents of writings in the organization's possession. That's why all notices and other writings should be placed in the appropriate lease file. In the case of hands-on properties, the person preparing an estoppel should be aware of whatever the one or two people involved have heard. On the other hand, a multi-location tenant, by example, shouldn't be considered as being "aware of" or "knowing" something that was said to a low-level store employee.

For those reasons, except in the most unique circumstances, a fair and accurate representation as to the default status of the other party would be: "We are not aware that the [other party to the lease] is currently in default of its obligations under the Lease and we have received no writing from anyone saying that the [other party to the lease] is currently in default of its obligations under the Lease."

The most commonly seen qualifier, modifier or weasel words all include some form of: "To our knowledge." Other formulations include the infamous, "To the <u>best</u> of our knowledge" or "To the best of our knowledge and belief." If those formulations make the certificate giver feels better, go right ahead and offer them up. Basically, "To the best of our knowledge" only sounds stronger; the word "best" doesn't add anything. Further, statements are always to the giver's "belief" even if that belief is wrong. If the party didn't "believe" what it was certifying, then it isn't being honest, and it shouldn't be making that particular certification. What matters is whether the certifying party has an obligation to "investigate" or merely to respond to the request for an estoppel letter based on what already is known by the organization at the time the estoppel letter is prepared. If no investigation is made, then as to those representations that properly are qualified by "knowledge," it would be appropriate to say, "To our knowledge, without any duty of investigation...." Certainly, the certificate recipient would prefer seeing: "To the best of our knowledge after due inquiry and investigation ...," but unless the agreement that requires a party to deliver the estoppel also requires the certifying party to conduct an investigation, there is no duty to do so.

More Qualifications: Duty to Investigate: Yes or No?

The conflict between having a duty to investigate and having no duty to investigate really applies to large organizations where information is decentralized and where there are many, many employees who might know "something." While it would be inappropriate for a single store tenant whose business is run by one or two individuals to assert a "no duty to investigate" qualification, the same would not be true for a wide-spread chain of retail stores. A reasonable compromise for a large tenant or a large landlord would be to define knowledge as being limited to what is known by its lease administration department, its accounting department, and its field manager for the store or property. Of course, each organization would have a different list and specific questions might call for the knowledge of a particular individual or department, as might be the case for representations about construction matters.

Where the representation is of the "here is the response to your due diligence request" type as contrasted with the "you can treat this as the truth" type, all anyone should expect is a statement as to what is currently known. It doesn't seem appropriate for anyone to think that the certificate giver should make a representation about something it doesn't really (or fully) know about. Because one should know whether all tenant improvement monies have been received or whether any written notices have been received, it isn't improper to expect an unqualified representation one way or the other. In contrast, it is almost impossible to be sure that: "No event has occurred, which with the giving of notice or the passage of time or both would constitute a default by Landlord under the Lease."

For statements like that, all one should be obligated to "say" is what one actually knows. If one actually knows that such an event has occurred (or that there is presently an uncured default), it should be revealed. A certifying party should not be required to represent something of which it is unaware and can't readily determine. Even though the recipient of a certificate is entitled to honest, non-quibbling representations, it isn't entitled to a "guaranty" from the certifying party as to items that the certifying party really isn't expected to fully know.

Qualifications aren't an all or nothing proposition. For example, if factually correct, an estoppel could properly state: "We have received no written notice from any governmental or quasi-governmental entity concerning an uncured violation of law by us relating to the leased space and, without undertaking any duty of investigation, we are unaware of any uncured violations of law by us relating to the leased space."

Reliance

A party may be willing to let a lender, buyer or prospective assignee rely on the statements in the estoppel, but not extend the same benefit to its own landlord or tenant. For example, a tenant may take the risk of mistakenly certifying to a prospective lender or purchaser that it has no claims against its current landlord, but be unwilling to let its landlord rely on such a mistaken certification. It is one thing for a tenant to lose a claim against the buyer of a property if the tenant mistakenly states that it has received all of the tenant improvement money owed to it by its landlord, but another to lose that same claim against its landlord who should have known better and who would be getting a windfall. So, by example, tenants may want to remove any text in the requested estoppel that says the statements are enforceable by the landlord. Even if no such text was included in the request, one could expressly state that: "This certificate may be relied on by third parties, but not by Landlord."

Hidden Lease Amendments

At times, an estoppel might be combined with or be a part of a subordination, non-disturbance, and attornment (SNDA) agreement. The "rules" for the "estoppel" portion of such a combined document are no different than a stand-alone estoppel. On the other hand, an estoppel should not be used to amend the lease itself. That's not what parties agreed the lease's estoppel provision was meant to accomplish. Further, estoppels are easily overlooked when reviewing the terms of a lease. Unfortunately, many estoppels submitted by one party to the other include "hidden" lease modifications. One common example is a provision that might say: "No rent has been or will be paid more than one month in advance." That's a lease amendment if the lease doesn't already say that no rent will be paid more than one month in advance. Certificate givers, in almost all circumstances, should strike such provisions from an estoppel. If the modification is agreed-upon and is appropriate, memorialize it in a more obvious way.

Take-Aways

There are two remaining observations. The first is that the fundamental effect of an estoppel is to shift certain risks to the certifying party and away from the certificate's recipient. The certifying party is obligated to "stand behind" what it represents. There's nothing wrong with that. That's what the marketplace for real property leases expects; the marketplace needs estoppels to work; it is part of the "deal" when one is a landlord or a tenant. So, certifying parties must be truthful. They need to avoid the risk of wrongly certifying as to "facts" that they really "own," such as to whether they are owed money. In contrast, they shouldn't be liable for making statements with a good faith, earnest belief in their truth when the actually "truth" is not fully knowable. That's what qualifications are for – to make a statement truthful.

The other observation is the estoppel process starts with the lease. It establishes the rules for what must be in an estoppel and what qualifications may properly be made. Attention must be paid to each lease's "estoppel certificate" provision; parties shouldn't be indifferent and leave it for the implementation stage for the issues to be resolved.

Chapter 20
HOW TO CREATE A
SIMPLIFIED WORDING
VERSION OF THE LEASE

Commercial real estate leases can be intimidating to anyone who does not read and deal with them on a daily basis.

So here is a tip to cut through the convoluted wording when reading the lease or creating a simplified version of the lease for use by others who may have to refer to the lease from time to time. But keep in mind that every word in the lease has meaning and the 'true lease' is the only lease that should be relied upon if a question or issue arises, not the simplified one we are about to create.

STEP 1
Always get or make a *duplicate copy* of the fully signed lease. The original should be

kept in a safe place. It is the **ONLY** version that should be referenced if an issue comes up, because it is the 'legal' copy. The second copy is the one that can become a quick reference guide to the lease. You will make a condensed version of the original lease highlighting the key point in each clause, using the copy.

STEP 2

On the duplicate copy **ONLY**, highlight the main essence of each clause, so that when reading the clause the main point you need to refer to in the management of your lease on a daily basis is highlighted.

Here is an example from a retail property lease concerning the need to keep store sales information. Here is the original wording as contained in the lease:

That the Tenant shall make and keep on the Premises for a period of at least two (2) years from the end of the Lease Year to which they are applicable or, if an audit is required or a controversy should arise between the parties hereto regarding Rent payable hereunder, then until such audit or controversy is terminated, correct permanent sales records (indicating daily sales reports) in accordance with good accounting and retail practice, which shall be open to the inspection and audit of the Landlord or its duly appointed representative at all reasonable times.

Believe it or not, that is just one sentence. To fully understand how difficult that is to read I put the text through a readability assessment. This assessment uses various tests to determine what grade level you must have to easily comprehend what is written. Scores over 22 should generally be taken to mean graduate level text while most newspapers and non-technical books write for a grade 4 reading level.

How did this fair?

Readability Formula	Grade
Flesch-Kincaid Grade Level	22.2
Gunning-Fog Score	25.9
Coleman-Liau Index	12.7
SMOG Index	16.3
Automated Readability Index	25.3
Average Grade Level	**20.5**

These tests indicate that this one clause could be easily understood by a person reading at a PhD level. No wonder leases intimidate people.

Now read that clause again. But this time pick out the most basic intent of the clause. You can either underline the important text or highlight it with a highlighting pen. But remember that if you make further copies of highlighted text, the highlighted portions may turn black depending on the colour of highlighter used.

How do you do that without having a PhD to understand the clause in the first place?

Use the **Who, What, When** method.

Almost all lease clauses provide direction to **someone** to do **something** by **some time.** To simplify the wording - for everyday needs – highlight Who must take action, What that action is and When is must be done.

Here is what you get:

That the **Tenant shall** make and **keep** on the Premises **for** a period of at least **two (2) years from the end of the Lease Year** to which they are applicable or, if an audit is required or a controversy should arise between the parties hereto regarding Rent payable hereunder, then until such audit or controversy is terminated, correct permanent **sales records** (indicating daily sales reports) in accordance with good accounting and retail practice, **which shall be open to** the **inspection and audit** of the Landlord or its duly appointed representative at all reasonable times.

And now the score is:

Readability Formula	Grade
Flesch-Kincaid Grade Level	8.8
Gunning-Fog Score	11.6
Coleman-Liau Index	8
SMOG Index	6
Automated Readability Index	10.1
Average Grade Level	**8.9**

There is certainly a lot more in the original clause than in the simplified, pared down version, such as where the documents should be kept, how they should be formatted, etc. But anyone reading the highlighted copy for the daily management of the lease will know that, in most circumstances, the tenant must keep sales records for two years after each lease year and those records may be audited by the landlord.

This isn't a substitution for the exact lease wording and an understanding of both the business and legal aspects of the original wording. It is however, a quick guide to gaining a basic understanding of the lease requirements for the day to day needs and for explaining a clause to someone who doesn't work with leases on a daily basis.

Always remember that the lease is written from two perspectives.

The first is the legal perspective. That is why we have long complicated clauses as lawyers attempt to minimize risk by including as many specifics as possible over as many potential situations as possible.

The second is the business perspective. The lease is the ongoing contract between the landlord and the tenant, so it must cover how that relationship will work over the time of the lease. This is a completely separate way of looking at the lease as compared to the legal point of view.

About Our Contributors

Chapter 1: The Lease Administrator by
Dominica Jamieson

Dominica Jamieson is a seasoned Lease
Administrator, specializing in Lease
interpretation, Lease audits, Lease
processes, Lease Lifecycle Management and
Lease documentation. As a certified Law
Clerk with 27 years experience in the Real
Estate industry, Dominica has gained vast
knowledge and experience in all areas of
Lease Administration, including Tenant's
and Landlord's Work, Construction and
Project Management. Her natural ability to
mentor, paired with training as a Certified
Business and Life Coach has assisted her in
successfully mentoring many junior lease
administrators into successful senior
positions.

Chapter 2: The Role of the Lease
Administrator by Mary Cook

Chapter 4: The Lease Administrator &
Accounting by Mary Cook

Mary Cook is Senior Lease Analyst with
CH2M Hill Facilities Services. Ms. Cook has
diversified experience in commercial real
estate property accounting, lease

administration, management, marketing, and lease drafting. Ms. Cook's experience includes working with both direct and third party disputes and has had great success whether working with tenants, CPAs, landlords, property managers, lease administrators or attorneys. She has negotiated leases and performs lease language review.

Chapter 5: Lease Abstraction by Mili Mezei

Mili Mezei, is a paralegal who started working in a real estate law firm and also become a Commissioner of Oaths and holds a real estate license. Mili has worked with Tenants, Landlords, Lenders, Land Development, Franchising, Facility Management and Property Management. During this time, Mili also obtained her real estate license, specializing in commercial properties. She is the owner of The Canadian Lease Abstractor, a firm specializing in providing quality lease abstracts for owners and tenants that simplify the lease and provides important financial and timing information.

Nandakumar Vedachalam is currently Assistant Manager at Integrand Analytics, Gurgaon, India and is responsible for managing Lease Administration Projects. He has a bachelor's degree in computer engineering from Vel's Srinivasa College of Eng. & Tech., affiliated to Anna University, Chennai, India. He started his professional career in 2009, as an Analyst, and worked on multiple Lease Projects in Commercial Real Estate Nandakumar has expertise in Lease Abstraction, Lease Audit, Financial Audit, CAM Audit and Year End Reconciliations. He has worked in both India and in the USA, on a project basis.

Ana Lopes, CLO is a certified leasing officer and has over 20 years of experience in legal services relating to commercial real estate and lease administration. Ana has worked with Canada Life Assurance Company, SNC-Lavalin, Toronto, Colliers International, and Allied REIT where she is currently Director,

Lease Administration, Central & Western Canada

Chapter 8: Lease Commencement Provisions by Howard Kline, Esq.

Howard Kline, has been involved in commercial real estate for over 39 years as an attorney, broker, arbitrator and also radio show host and founder of CRE Radio & TV (CREradio.com), since December 2010.

Over the years, Mr. Kline has worked as General Counsel and Director of Real Estate for a national user of office, R & D and retail space, utilizing both his legal and brokerage licenses, and General Counsel for a major regional supermarket chain that owned its own shopping centers. As an attorney, he also practiced law as outside counsel to many major commercial landlords doing lease transactional work and lease litigation, including unlawful detainers and rent collections. As a real estate salesperson, he served as a tenant rep in New York City and as a broker for numerous lease transactions throughout the United States.

Chapter 11: What Are Recoveries? By Wendy Engel Murphey

Wendy Engel Murphey has over 25 years of experience as a lease administrator. She has extensive and thorough knowledge of commercial, retail and industrial leasing, including mixed-use, from letters of intent to lease execution through lease renewal and/or termination, and all aspects in between. In addition she is experienced in budgeting, reforecasting and recovery reconciliation. Wendy earned a RPA designation from BOMA. Ms. Murphey lives and works in the Washington, DC metropolitan area.

Chapter 19: Estoppels by Ira Meislik, Esq

Ira Meislik is a principal at the Montclair, New Jersey law firm of Meislik & Meislik. His practice is concentrated in two areas Business Law and Commercial Real Estate Law. Mr. Meislik's commercial real estate practice focuses on the needs of landlords and tenants primarily within shopping centers and office properties. In addition to crafting space and ground leases, he has extensive experience in the acquisition, disposition, and financing of real property. He is a Fellow of the American College of Real Estate Lawyers and one of seven members of the Uniform Law Commission's Joint Editorial Board (JEB) for Uniform Real Property Acts.

<u>All other Chapters</u> by Peter D. Morris

Peter D. Morris CRX, SCLS, SCSM, SCMD is the founder of the Greenstead Consulting Group and is a certified and recognized retail property expert holding multiple senior accreditations in the leasing, management and marketing of retail properties. In a career that has spanned more than three decades, Mr. Morris has worked globally in 8 countries and lived in three to bring a unique global perspective. He has worked with institutional owners such as Cadillac Fairview and Brookfield Properties and was the Chief Operating Officer of Partners Real Estate Investment Trust; as well as in a third party capacity as Senior Vice President with Colliers International. Previously, he was a retailer so he provides a 360^0 view of a negotiation. He is also the author of the book <u>Masterguide to Leasing for Retail Landlords.</u>

The Greenstead Consulting Group (GreensteadCG.com) provides consulting and training programs on a global scale.

Praise for
Masterguide to Leasing for Retail Landlords
By: Peter D. Morris

Masterguide to Leasing for Retail Landlords™ e-book provides proven best practices in four areas of the lease negotiation, the latest trends in leases and little known techniques to enhance revenues while reducing risk.

This 261 page book provides hands-on, practical advice and not just theory or general business concepts. It contains wisdom gained from administering to thousands of leases crafted by dozens of North America's leading landlords and tenants.

Who should buy this e-book?
Asset managers, leasing agents, property managers, lease administrators, paralegals, accountants, and anyone else interested in improving the value to retail properties. Those new to the industry will gain the equivalent of decades of knowledge, while industry veterans will gain fresh, new insights.

Here is what the industry says about the **Masterguide to Leasing for Retail Landlords** e-book:

As a former senior real estate executive for a brand name retailer, I can say that retailers don't want landlords to learn these negotiating strategies.

Mark Taylor B.Comm, CPM Vice President, Real Estate (Retired)

A very good and very readable book. More importantly, it fills a real void in the literature. And coming from someone with Mr. Morris' credentials and experience, it has a lot of credibility.

John S. Andrew, Ph.D. Director, Queen's Real Estate Roundtable; Continuing Adjunct Assistant Professor, School of Urban & Regional Planning & School of Business, Queen's University

Anyone who wants to create value and reduce risk through deal making in today's rapidly evolving retail market will want this book and keep it handy. Peter leverages his cross-functional experience, drawing from real events and provides practical, value-add techniques and insight to the science of retail leasing.

George Chambers, CCIM, CPM,RPA Woodland Chambers Group

Masterguide to Leasing for Retail Landlords is a must-read for anyone involved in or thinking of becoming involved in the landlord

side of leasing. The author, Peter Morris, is obviously an expert on retail leasing. His expertise is reflected in this manual, which in my opinion should be read by every landlord. Rather than reinvent the wheel, why not learn from the expert?
Craig Patterson B.COMM., LL.B.
Editor in Chief, RETAIL INSIDER

Preview the first chapter for free at
www.vantageknowledge.com/for-landlords

Also available through Amazon.com in print and Kindle versions.

www.ingramcontent.com/pod-product-compliance
Lightning Source LLC
Chambersburg PA
CBHW061239220326
41599CB00028B/5476